Zero to Everyone

The Marketing Playbook to Become Visible in the Marketplace

Akash Jaiswal

ISBN 979-8-89133-859-3

Dedication

To my Grandfather and Grandmother,

Your stories and wisdom lit the spark of my imagination, teaching me the value of tradition and the beauty of dreams. Your love transcends time, guiding and inspiring me always. This book is a tribute to that enduring love.

To my Father,

Your resilience and integrity have been my compass, teaching me the true measure of success. Your unwavering support and sacrifices are the bedrock of my aspirations. This book reflects your faith in me, a faith that has shaped my path.

To my Mother,

Your compassion and unconditional love have been my sanctuary. You taught me the power of kindness and the wisdom in simplicity. This book mirrors your nurturing spirit, a guiding light in my life.

To my beloved family, you are the unsung heroes of my story. "Zero to Everyone" is as much yours as it is mine, a celebration of your values, sacrifices, and belief in me. In dedicating this book to you, I honor the legacy you've given me, a legacy of love and wisdom.

With all my love and deepest gratitude,

Akash Jaiswal

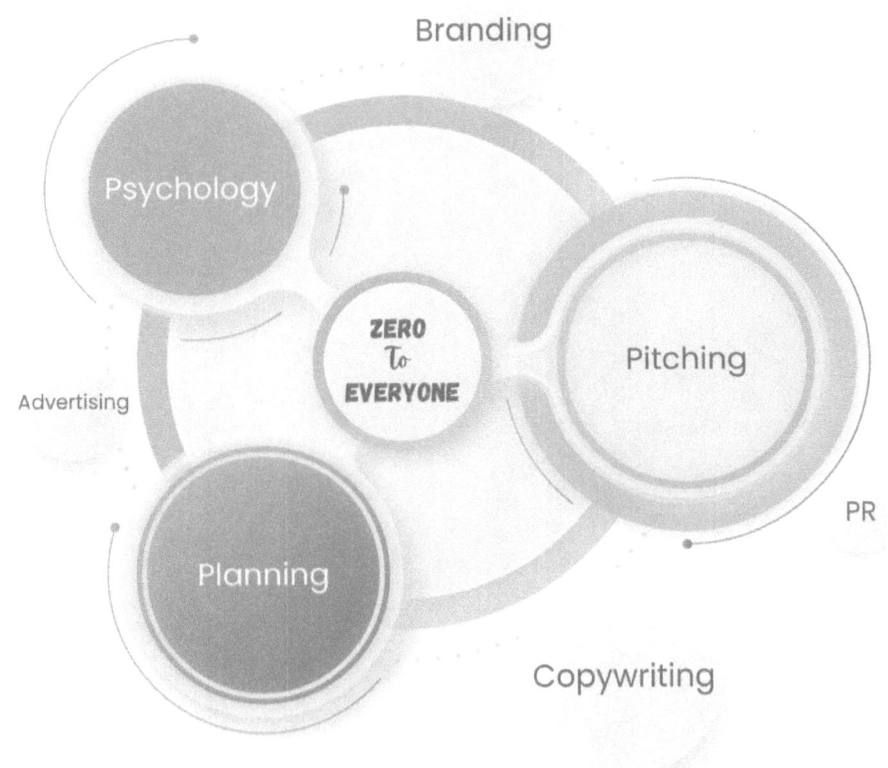

Get ready to explore the Marketing Ecosystem…

Go from "Zero to Everyone"

Contents

3. Advertising — **103**

4. Copywriting Methods — **119**

5. Player BECOMES a Product: The AIR JORDAN Case Study — **151**

6. Go-To-Market Plan — **159**

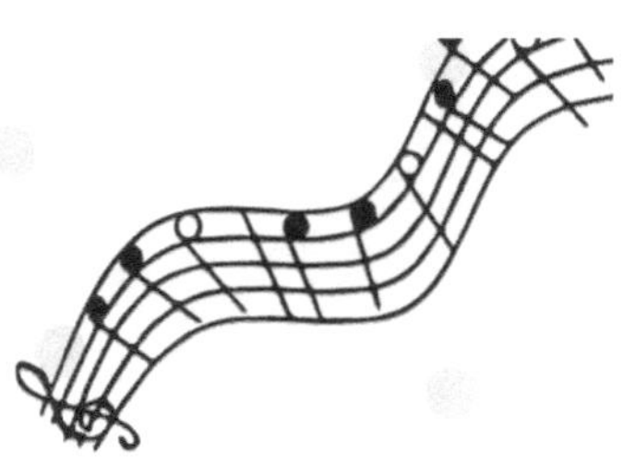

PrEFaCE

Preface

"Zero to Everyone" is not just a book; it's a conversation. A dialogue between you and me, where I am sharing insights from the trenches of marketing, and you are embarking on a journey from obscurity to ubiquity. Whether you're an entrepreneur, a marketer, or simply someone intrigued by the art of reaching everyone, this book is your compass in the vast, often tumultuous ocean of marketing.

Imagine a world where your product or service resonates with every individual's needs and wants. A world where your brand isn't just a name, but a narrative woven into the lives of your consumers. "Zero to Everyone" is your guide to creating that world. It's about understanding that we all harbor a three-year-old child within us, curious, eager, and waiting to be enthralled. Your marketing journey begins with tapping into that universal sentiment.

At its core, marketing is a philosophy – a philosophy where organizational goals are not just met but exceeded by understanding and satisfying the needs and wants of your target market. This book is designed to be your one-stop solution for all things marketing. It's about building a moat in the market, not just to protect your territory but to expand it.

"Zero to Everyone" delves deep into the functions of marketing. From the critical role of Research & Development in understanding your audience to the nuances of Branding that give your product its unique identity. You'll learn about the intricacies of Pricing, the art of Promotion, the logistics of Physical Distribution, and much more. Each function is a cog in the wheel of successful marketing, and understanding them is key to mastering the market.

The Journey Through the Chapters

The book is structured to take you through various facets of marketing, each a chapter, each a new realm of knowledge:

Psychology in Marketing: Explore the evolution of the brain, the cocktail of chemicals that drive consumer behavior, and why we buy what we buy.

Understand the science behind shopping and the psychological techniques that influence pricing.

Branding: This chapter is about the narrative beyond the product. Learn how luxury brands enchant their audience and how you can use these strategies to differentiate your brand.

Advertising: Discover what makes an ad effective, unleash your creative genius, and understand the laws of powerful advertising tailored for different markets.

Copywriting Methods: Uncover the secrets of impactful copywriting, from crafting resonant words to understanding the Problem-Agitate-Solution formula.

Case Studies: Dive into case studies like the AIR JORDAN saga to understand how players become products.

Go-To-Market Plan: Learn about targeting niches, identifying your audience, crafting your message, and much more.

Connecting Brand with Rituals: Understand the importance of integrating your brand into the daily rituals of your consumers.

Learnings from Superfans: Discover how to create fans, not just customers, for your product.

Pitching Tactics: Master the art of optimizing your deals and pitches.

Public Relations and Image Building: Learn how to manage your public image and relations effectively.

"Zero to Everyone" is more than just a collection of strategies and theories. It's a narrative filled with real-life examples, practical advice, and a deep understanding of what makes marketing work. It's about making complex concepts understandable, breaking down sophisticated strategies into actionable steps, and guiding you through every phase of your marketing journey.

As you turn these pages, remember, this is a conversation. I'm not just imparting knowledge; I'm inviting you to question, to ponder, and to apply these insights in your unique context. This book is a dialogue where your perspective, your challenges, and your aspirations are as crucial as the words written here.

You are about to embark on a journey from zero to everyone. It's a path filled with challenges, surprises, and immense rewards. "Zero to Everyone" is your companion on this journey, a guide that will help you navigate the complex world of marketing with ease and confidence.

Welcome to "Zero to Everyone" – where your journey from obscurity to ubiquity begins. Let's turn the page and start this exciting adventure together.

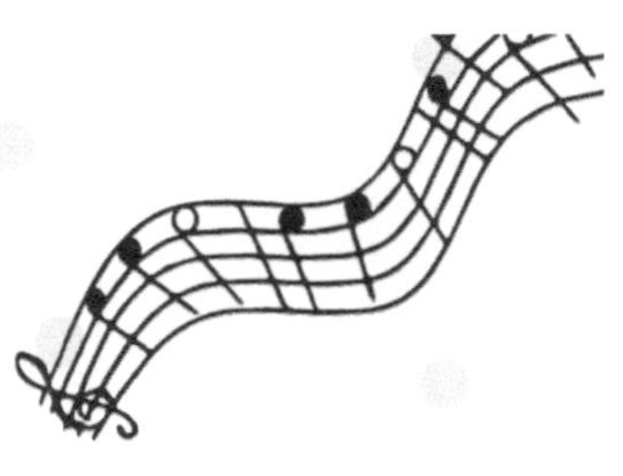

PSYCHOLOGY

1. Psychology in Marketing

1.1 Brain Evolution its Evolution Over Time

"The best marketing doesn't feel like marketing."

— Tom Fishburne

Why am I putting this chapter at the very beginning? It is because many new marketing products fail because we do not realize how our own brain works. After reading tons of books, I realized it was high time to reveal the secrets and functioning of the brain, and later you can learn how to bypass those. Marketing really means getting into the brains of your audience, and they are ready to buy your product. If you are not getting sales with the right marketing, then that means there is a gap between the message you are sending and the message they are receiving.

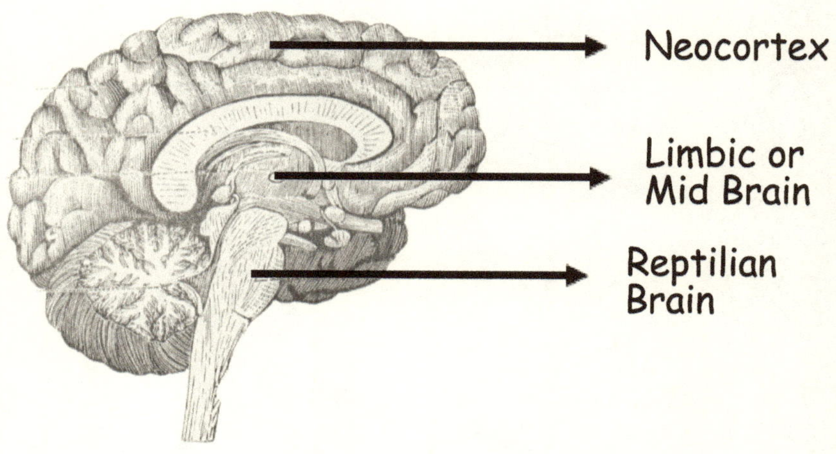

The better you are at keeping the attention of your audience, the more likely he/she will be to buy your product. We always learn from our parents or our teachers that whenever you are having a problem, go back to the situation from where it started. It means we should always know history to make changes in the present. You can see such things happening in politics a lot. What does a politician do? He quotes what was working and what needed to be changed, using basic examples from freedom fighters or any timeline where everyone was happy.

So let's first understand a bit about human evolution, and then we will jump on to the brain's evolution.

- **Australopithecus (4-2 million years ago):** Early hominids walked upright and had a brain size similar to chimpanzees.

- **Homo habilis (2.4-1.5 million years ago):** The first to show significant brain enlargement and use of stone tools.

- **Homo erectus (1.8 million-300,000 years ago):** Exhibited further brain growth and was the first to use fire and complex tools.

- **Neanderthals (400,000-40,000 years ago):** Close relatives of modern humans, with a brain size even larger than ours, but they eventually became extinct.

- **Homo sapiens (around 300,000 years ago to present):** Modern humans, characterized by a larger brain (especially the neocortex), complex language, and the ability to create art and engage in scientific and philosophical thought.

The human brain's evolution is a fascinating journey that spans millions of years. It's typically divided into three main parts: the reptilian brain, the limbic system (mid-brain), and the neocortex. Each of these parts evolved at different times and serves distinct functions.

Reptilian Brain (Brainstem and Basal Ganglia):

- **Evolution:** The oldest part of the human brain, the reptilian brain, evolved around 500 million years ago. It's similar to the brain present in reptiles and other ancient animals. It is located at the back of our heads, which are responsible for the automatic or unconscious functions of the brain, and it has habits ingrained in it.

- **Function:** This part of the brain is responsible for our most basic survival functions, such as heart rate, breathing, body temperature regulation, and balance. It's also involved in behaviors related to aggression, dominance, territoriality, and ritual displays. Basically, it is involved in filtering messages and has strong basic emotions like the "fight or flight" response. Its basic function is to keep us alive.

Limbic System (Mid-Brain):

- **Evolution:** The limbic system began to develop in the first mammals, about 150-200 million years ago. It's more sophisticated than the reptilian brain and provides mammals with a greater range of emotions and behaviors.

- **Function:** The limbic system is responsible for our emotional life and has a lot to do with the formation of memories. Key components include the amygdala (emotional reactions like fear and anger), hippocampus (memory and navigation), and hypothalamus (hormonal control, appetite, and other homeostatic systems). It has significance in decision but it has no capacity for language, which determines the meaning of things and social situations.

Neocortex:

- **Evolution:** The neocortex is the most recent evolution of the brain, significantly developed in primates and especially in humans. It started to evolve around 2-3 million years ago with the emergence of early hominids.

- **Function:** The neocortex is involved in higher-order brain functions such as sensory perception, cognition, generation of motor commands, spatial reasoning, and language. In humans, it's highly developed and allows for complex problem-solving, abstract thinking, planning, and culture. Rational and analytical thought and interpretation of language come from this.

The evolution of the brain, particularly the development of the neocortex, is closely linked to these stages of human evolution, reflecting the increasing complexity of behaviors and cognitive abilities in our ancestors.

The reptilian brain reacts first for immediate survival; the limbic system then processes the emotional aspects; and finally, the neocortex provides a conscious, rational understanding and response to the stimulus. This layered response exemplifies how our brain's evolution contributes to a comprehensive reaction to stimuli in our environment.

Let's illustrate how a message or stimulus travels through the different parts of the brain—from the reptilian brain to the limbic system (mid-brain), and then to the neocortex—using a real-life example: hearing a sudden, loud noise.

Sequence of Brain Response to a Sudden Loud Noise:

Initial Stimulus: A loud noise, like a car backfiring or a door slamming shut.

Reptilian Brain Response:

Immediate Reaction: The sound is first processed by the reptilian brain.

Survival Mechanism: This part of the brain quickly assesses if the noise is a threat. It triggers an instantaneous, involuntary reaction, often known as the "startle reflex."

Physical Response: Your heart rate may increase, and your muscles might tense up, preparing your body for a potential "fight or flight" response.

Limbic System Response:

Emotional Processing: Almost immediately after the reptilian brain's response, the limbic system starts to process the emotional content of the stimulus.

Fear or Anxiety: If the sound is perceived as threatening or startling, the amygdala (part of the limbic system) activates, generating feelings of fear or anxiety.

Memory Recall: The hippocampus, another part of the limbic system, might associate this sound with past experiences, influencing your emotional response.

Neocortex Response:

Conscious Awareness and Analysis: The neocortex then engages to consciously process and analyze the sound.

Rationalization: It helps you understand that the noise was just a car backfiring and not something dangerous.

Decision Making: Based on this analysis, the neocortex helps in deciding the next course of action, like calming yourself down or simply acknowledging the noise and moving on.

Social and Contextual Understanding: It also allows you to comprehend the social context (e.g., realizing it's a common city sound) and modulate your response accordingly.

This behaviour applies to real world pitching your product as well. Here pitching I mean is marketing to wide audience at a single time. Here are three things that you must by-heart remember when you are trying to market your offer or product to your audience's brain:

1. If there is no DANGER ⟶ Reptilian brain will ignore it [90% of message will get discarded before it is passed onto mid brain then neocortex]

2. If there is no EXCITEMENT ⟶ Reptilian brain will ignore it

3. If there is no URGENCY ⟶ Reptilian brain will ignore it

Do not try to overcomplicate things by being more creative reptilian brain is going to ignore it. With advancing days our attention is going into pit. Recent studies reveal that the average human attention span has dwindled to just 8.25 seconds, a significant decrease of nearly 25% since 2000, now even shorter than the 9-second attention span of a goldfish.

This decline highlights a notable shift in our ability to focus, underscoring the challenges in an increasingly digital and fast-paced world. With this let's move onto our next most important topic to be covered if we want to have hold on marketing today

1.1.1 Cocktail of Chemicals: Mental Mechanism

"Marketing is no longer about the stuff that you make, but about the stories you tell."

– Seth Godin

Do you know what different hormones the brain secretes for you?

I am guessing you might now know all. Am I correct, or am I correct? I will give you some information about the hormone; some of it you might have heard too.

- **Serotonin:** regulates mood, appetite, and sleep.

- **Dopamine:** Involved in the reward and pleasure centers of the brain, as well as movement and motivation.

- **Oxytocin:** Promotes social bonding, trust, and attachment.

- **Cortisol:** Regulates stress response and the body's metabolism.

- **Adrenaline (epinephrine):** Involved in the "fight or flight" response and increases heart rate and blood pressure.

- **Melatonin:** Regulates the sleep-wake cycle.

- **Endorphins:** Natural painkillers that are released during exercise or other activities.

- **Growth hormone:** Stimulates cell growth, reproduction, and regeneration.

- **Thyroid hormones:** Regulate metabolism and energy levels in the body.

- **Estrogen and testosterone:** Regulate sexual development and reproductive function.

This information might have blown your mind away. Considering you are a normal human being like me, I will let you know why the above information is important when you are building a brand.

Have some patience!

After all, all brands are mere images and perceptions in our brains. There are many brain operating principles that influence and drive behavior. Here are a few examples:

- **Reward system:** The brain's reward system is responsible for motivating behavior by associating certain actions or experiences with pleasure or positive outcomes.

- **Emotions:** The brain's emotional system plays a key role in driving behavior by shaping our feelings and reactions to different stimuli.

- **Learning and memory:** The brain's ability to learn and remember information is a major driver of behavior, as our experiences shape our understanding of the world and inform our decisions and actions.

- **Perception and attention:** The brain's ability to perceive and attend to different stimuli influences behavior by determining what information we prioritize and respond to.

- **Executive function:** The brain's executive function system helps us plan, organize, and make decisions, which influences our behavior by shaping our ability to pursue goals and engage in complex tasks.

- **Social cognition:** The brain's social cognition system enables us to understand and navigate social situations, which influences behavior by shaping our interactions with others.

- **Stress response:** The brain's stress response system influences behavior by shaping our reactions to challenging or threatening situations and can trigger fight, flight, or freeze responses.

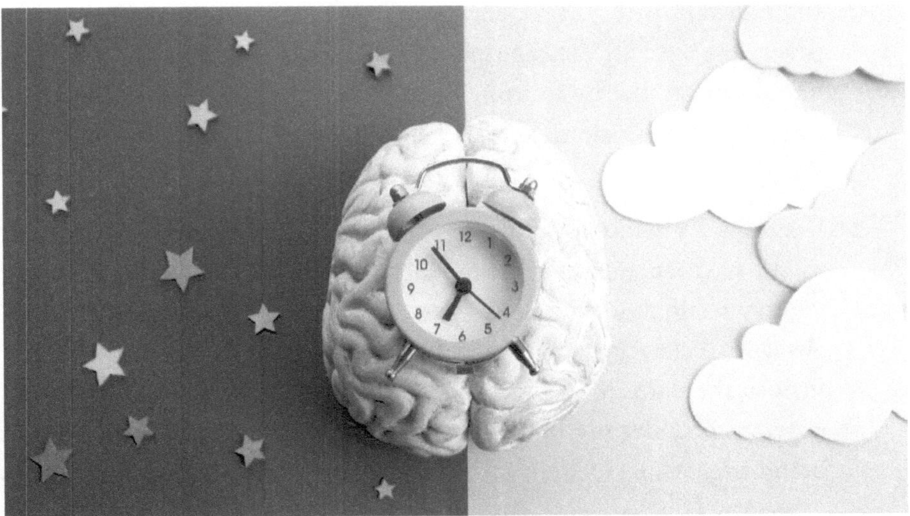

There was a lady who kept buying this shampoo. The brand of shampoo claimed that it would make hair stronger and shinier. She, after seeing the advertisement, went on to buy it. After utilizing that for a month, she realized that her hair had not stopped falling and that its thickness had reduced. As hair is part of women's beauty, she was worried and went to check on the clinic, where she found out that shampoo was causing more damage.

Her doctor recommended some other shampoo and assured her that this would make her hair healthy and fine. As human beings, we want to feel good and avoid pain. Without even thinking, she followed her doctor's instructions, whatever the brand.

We learned that brands affect our behaviour. Your brand needs to make people feel safe so that they will spread the word about you.

According to professor Arvind Sahay, there are five main brain operations that a brand could make use of in developing something new or moving forward with something they already have. [More, we will discuss in Branding section]

1. The brain wants to feel good, to avoid pain, to feel secure, to get rewards, and so on. Obviously, our serotonin and dopamine levels will go up as we feel good about ourselves. The key here is how does brand make me and your customers feel safer?

2. Brain always tries to save energy all the time. It does so by pushing processing into unconsciousness, and it runs in automatic mode. A brand can do that by forming a habit. The brain conserves energy by using habit formation. The goal of branding should be to make the brand habitual.

3. Brain always looks for patterns, groups, and categories. I know you might have encountered many things on a day to day basis where you try to link everything to something. Like when you see red, you always associate it with energy, fire courage, etc. A brand can better fit into the pattern by asking questions like, Is there a pattern in the experience? Does my brand fit into that experience pattern? A loved brand triggers oxytocin in the brain and can increase adoption.

4. Brain remembers and engages contrasts/differences/peak shifts from existing patterns; contrasts excite the brain. It increases dopamine in the brain. It keeps brands new and novel. It is a generally unexpected pattern. You can call it an element of surprise. Amul brand keeps on creating new cartoons related to burning topics. So a brand that helps to create a dopamine spike that is higher than those provided by competition will be liked by the brain and move into memory.

5. Brains designed to mirror, to conform socially with others, and to interact with people, animals, and objects around us. It makes us feel secure. This makes us feel part of the community. Already, many brands are exploiting this human urge to conform and imitate. As an example, you might want to be an Apple user to be a part of the community.

1.2 Neuromarketing + Psychology + Neuroscience: Consumer Do Not Think What They Feel

"People don't buy what you do; they buy why you do it."

– Simon Sinek

What is neuromarketing?

If you have been with me till now, that means you find topics about the brain and psychology fascinating. Now we are going to look into some aspects where scientists used BIG MACHINES to find out our subconscious activity that we ourselves do not know.

Imagine combining the intricate workings of the brain with the dynamic world of marketing; that's neuromarketing for you. It delves deep into your subconscious, uncovering your hidden preferences, motivations, and expectations, offering a crystal ball into your behavior as a consumer. Think of it not as a replacement but as a powerful ally to traditional marketing, bringing unique insights that truly resonate with you.

Using EEG and MRI [Magnetic Resonance Imaging] technologies to track brain electrical activity to learn how consumers feel and reply. It is measured with combined biometric measures such as heart rates, respiration rates, sweat levels, facial movements, and eye movements.

Did you know …… that in the early days of neuromarketing, a fascinating experiment by Read Montague revealed our hidden preferences between Coke and Pepsi? Picture this: participants, claiming a preference for Coke, surprisingly leaned towards Pepsi in a blind taste test, while their brain scans told an intriguing story. This eye-opener, highlighting Coke's superior marketing, shows how what you say and what you truly prefer can be worlds apart, proving just how powerful neuroscience can be in uncovering your real responses to marketing stimuli.

Similarly, you might have seen your bafflement with the PRICE TAGs too… Come on, don't lie if you haven't. The higher the price, the greater the liking.

Neuromarketing, used in conjunction with research, can be a game changer. I will give you some methods and the cost of them so that it can give you an overview. For startup owners, this can get a little bit overwhelming to just have a look and get to the next awesome topic.

Method	Level of Detail	Cost	Time	Expertise Required	Participant Compliance	Context Allowance	Setup Cost per Participant
fMRI	High	Very High	Long	High	Moderate	Low	High
EEG	Moderate	Moderate	Shorter	Moderate	High	Moderate	Lower than fMRI
Eye Tracking	Moderate	Lower	Short	Low to Moderate	High	High	Low
GSR	Low	Low	Short	Low	High	High	Very Low
Facial Coding	Moderate	Low to Moderate	Short	Moderate	High	High	Low

1.2.1 Stimuli to activate the Reptile Brain

"Success is not the key to happiness. Happiness is the key to success. If you love what you are doing, you will be successful."

— Albert Schweitzer

Even with so much evolution, our roots remain the same. That means how we respond and how we get thinking about something for too long, even without notice, we are spending time on that. If you master the art of these stimuli, then the long way of doing things will become easy.

Patrick Renvoise and Christophe Morin wrote a book called Neuromarketing about this in 2005. Our old brain drives decisions. So market to the old brain. The six triggers are:

1. Self-centered

2. Contrast

3. Tangible input

4. The beginning and the end

5. Visual stimuli

6. Emotion

Let's dive into the world of neuromarketing, where your brain plays a pivotal role in how you perceive and interact with brands. Here are six neuromarketing stimuli that speak directly to your 'old brain', each accompanied by a real-life example that you might find strikingly familiar:

Self-centered: We are all are SELFISH. The "ME" is the center of the old brain. So, you should make a message that can enter their ears about what you can do for them before they give you attention.

Think about how Apple markets its products. They don't just talk about the features; they show you how an iPhone or MacBook will enhance your life, tapping into your inner desire to make life easier and more enjoyable.

Contrast: We are very sensitive when we are compared to someone, right? Come on! When you didn't say it to me, you were never compared to Sharma Ji's son to get you motivated to study. Our old brain is sensitive to clear contrasts like danger/safety or high/low. We do pay attention when there is a change of state, or what we call DISRUPTIONS.

Ever noticed how insurance companies compare the dire consequences of being uninsured with the peace of mind their policies offer? This stark contrast is designed to make the decision clear and prompt you to act for your safety.

Tangible Input: I remember when I was in high school, my teacher made the history subject very heavy. They thought it was just information that students needed to grasp. Now, putting it scientifically, old brain is not qualified to process written language or the use of words, especially complicated ones. It will lead to more thinking and less action. So make your ideas easy and do not lay a burden of information.

IKEA catalogs are a great example. They don't just list furniture dimensions; they show you beautifully designed rooms, making it easy for you to imagine how that furniture would look in your own home.

The Beginning and the End: If I ask you what happened in the Harry Potter and the Prisoner of Azkaban movie, you will probably tell me the beginning part of how Harry's uncle was the villain and, at the end, how he saved them from his teacher. If you are more into the movie, you might also remember "Expecto Patronum.". But can you elaborate on a 3-hour movie? hell no.

The old brain enjoys openings and finales and often overlook middle part. So you need to place most important message at the beginning is a must and repeat the same at the end. We always want to win, and it can be as simple as predicting what someone is going to say or do because of the dopamine our mind makes. If you can disrupt that, you got attention.

Think about a memorable movie trailer or a compelling book blurb. They grab your attention at the start and leave you with a cliffhanger, ensuring you remember and yearn for more.

Visual Stimuli: If you know about human evolution, then you must know that we use visuals to communicate. The words and language came into being way later. Our optic nerve works 40 times faster than our auditory nerve. When you see danger, you are likely to run because of your reflexes, giving you less time to process information in the Neocortex.

Coca-Cola's vibrant ads feature happy, smiling people enjoying a Coke. These visuals are not just about the drink; they're about the joy and connection you feel, making you associate these positive emotions with the brand.

Emotion: We are not thinking machines that feel; we are feeling machines that think. This was well said by Antonio Damasio. We will remember events or situations much better when we have experienced them with strong emotions like love, anger, sadness, joy, or surprise.

Charity organizations often use emotional storytelling in their campaigns, showing real people with real struggles. This emotional connection makes you more likely to empathize and contribute.

Let's move on to the next amazing chapter…

1.2.2 Why do we BUY? Why... Why... Why...

"Marketing is no longer about the stuff you make, but about the stories you tell."

– Seth Godin

If I ask you, what have you bought today?

Come on! If you say no, then I would definitely not agree with you...... WHY?

Because you might have gotten those milk pouches for your Tea/Coffee. Or you might have gotten your Chai-sutta at the corner of your house. Or maybe some water bottles if you are travelling... etc. etc.

Believe me, you are not buying the products you need to fulfill your desires. And whichever is delivering the best desire, that product is in your house.

If you do not believe me, let's take the Milk packet you have in your fridge...... I am guessing "Amul". So you have taken that because you believe that milk is pure and well toned. And then drinking it will not harm you, which means your health will be maintained.

Or if you have a guest coming to your house, you want to serve them the best. We all know "अतिथि देवो भव।". So what you will see is that your social status is maintained, and you will not do anything that would harm that. This means you are trying to maintain your Social status or Relationships.

We know now that the world is evolving, and you have to tap into the core human desire to MARKET your product successfully. This creates motivation to buy, and you can shape your marketing strategy to connect on a deeper level.

In this chapter, we will explore how businesses can leverage the market by understanding and appealing to three core human desires: health, wealth, and relationships.

Every product is marketed based on three fundamental desires, or core markets: health, wealth, and relationships. When individuals make a purchase, they seek a desired outcome in at least one of these areas. While some products may cater to multiple desires, it is crucial to tailor the marketing message to emphasize one specific desire.

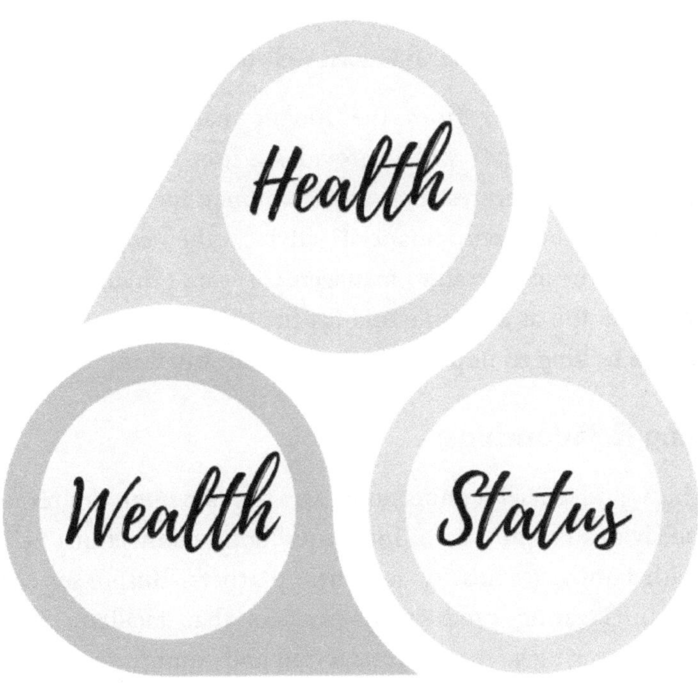

Leveraging Health:

Health is a fundamental desire shared by individuals across the globe. People strive for physical and mental well-being, and you can leverage this desire to connect with your target market. By offering products or services that promote health and wellness, companies can capture the attention and loyalty of health-conscious consumers.

For instance, consider a case study of "Organic Tattva", a company that manufactures organic food products. By highlighting the health benefits of their products, such as being free from harmful additives and supporting a balanced diet, they can resonate with health-conscious consumers. By emphasizing the positive impact on their well-being, they positioned themselves as a trusted brand that cares about its customers' health.

Leveraging Wealth:

Wealth, in terms of financial prosperity and security, is a core desire for many individuals. People seek opportunities to improve their financial situation and build wealth for themselves and their families. You can tap into this desire by offering products or services that help consumers achieve financial goals or enhance their financial well-being.

A real-life case study from the Indian market is that of a fintech company called "Phonepe" which provides a user-friendly mobile banking app. By highlighting features such as easy money management, investment options, and personalized financial advice, the company appeals to individuals' desire for wealth management and financial security. By positioning their app as a reliable tool for financial success, they can attract a large user base seeking to improve their financial situation.

Leveraging Relationships:

Relationships and social connections are fundamental desires that drive human behavior. People yearn for meaningful connections with others, be they with family, friends, or romantic partners. Businesses can leverage this desire by creating products or services that facilitate and enhance relationships, fostering a sense of connection and community.

Take the example of a social networking platform, "Instagram," which focuses on connecting individuals with shared interests. By providing features that encourage interaction, such as discussion forums, events, and user-generated content, the platform creates an environment where users can forge new relationships and deepen existing ones. By nurturing a sense of belonging and connection, the platform becomes an integral part of users' social lives.

Understanding and leveraging the core human desires of health, wealth, and relationships can significantly impact a business's success in the market. By aligning marketing strategies with these desires, companies can create a deep emotional connection with their target audience, foster brand loyalty, and drive growth.

It's important for you or your strategy to approach this process authentically and genuinely, providing value.

It's not just about exploiting desires but rather addressing genuine needs. Let's move on to the next amazing chapter…

1.2.3 The Science of Shopping - Designed for Humans

"Knowing is not enough; we must apply. Wishing is not enough;
we must do."

– Johann Wolfgang von Goethe

Do you know why you choose certain products when you go out to buy them? Well you will get answer of this. Just keep on…

Shopping is influenced by physical and anatomical factors. Stores designed with these in mind create a more pleasant and efficient shopping experience. For example, the placement of products at eye level or the arrangement of aisles can significantly impact your shopping behavior.

I am sure you know that tobacco's lethal impact is staggering. It claims the lives of over 8 million people annually, including around 1.3 million non-smokers exposed to second-hand smoke. Predominantly affecting low- and middle-income countries, tobacco use is a global health crisis, with up to half of its users dying from tobacco-related diseases.

The health warnings on cigarette packs are designed to deter smoking, but research shows they can inadvertently stimulate cravings by activating the brain's nucleus accumbens, known as the "craving spot." When smokers are exposed to health warnings, instead of being deterred, this area of the brain is activated, potentially increasing the desire to smoke. This counterintuitive response highlights a significant challenge in tobacco control efforts.

The implications for marketers and public health officials are profound. It suggests that traditional methods of deterrence, such as graphic health warnings, might not be as effective as previously thought. This calls for a reevaluation of strategies and the development of more nuanced approaches to combat tobacco use. Understanding the complex psychological and neurological responses to health warnings is crucial to designing more effective public health campaigns.

Innovative approaches that go beyond fear-based tactics are needed. It's a call to action for marketers and public health officials to evolve their strategies, employing more sophisticated and psychologically informed approaches to truly impact smoking behavior and ultimately save lives.

WHO on Health Warnings: Pictorial health warnings that include graphic, fear-arousing information have proven to be particularly effective in detracting from the overall attractiveness of tobacco products. Source: World Health Organization

Your brain is a sorting machine, constantly filtering information. Most of it becomes background noise, but some details stick, influencing your choices without you even realizing it. This process is unconscious and ongoing, shaping your preferences and decisions every day.

Sensory Influences on Shopping Behavior

Your senses play a crucial role in shopping. The smell of fresh bread in a supermarket, the sound of a familiar jingle, or the sight of a well-designed product can all sway your decisions. These sensory cues trigger emotional responses and memories, influencing your choices more than you might realize

The Power of Somatic Markers in Decision Making

Imagine you're walking into a men's room at a theater, expecting the usual scene. But then, you look up, and there it is - a lone plastic urinal, oddly perched seven feet high. Right beside it, the words "Spiderman 3… Coming Soon" catch your eye. Sony's a clever trick, right? It's not something you see every day, and that's exactly why it sticks in your mind. It makes you think about Spiderman in a whole new way, doesn't it?

When you shop, your brain uses somatic markers—emotional shortcuts based on past experiences—to make decisions. These markers guide you towards choices that feel right, even if they're not entirely rational. For example, you might choose Jif peanut butter because it evokes a sense of trust and quality, influenced by the brand's long-standing presence and marketing.

The Role of Rituals and Superstitions in Brand Loyalty

Products and brands associated with rituals or superstitions tend to be more memorable and appealing. In a fast-paced world, these rituals provide a sense of comfort and belonging. Being part of a brand community, like Apple or Netflix, offers a sense of security and connection.

The Impact of Sensory Branding

Sensory branding, which involves appealing to your senses beyond just sight, is becoming increasingly important. Smells and sounds can evoke stronger emotions. responses than visual cues alone, making them powerful tools in influencing your purchasing decisions.

Shopping is more than a transaction; it's an emotional experience. The joy of discovery, the satisfaction of a good deal, and the comfort of familiar rituals all contribute to the pleasure of shopping. Brands that understand and tap into these emotional aspects are more likely to win your loyalty and your dollars.

Men and women shop differently due to inherent behavioral tendencies. Men often shop with a purpose and make quicker decisions, while women enjoy the process of exploring and comparing. Understanding these differences can lead to more targeted and effective marketing strategies.

Let me give you some exciting statistics about the difference between men and women shopping:

- **Male vs Female Shopping Habits and Preferences:** This research provides an analysis of the latest available statistics on male vs female shopping behaviors, habits, and preferences by retail category and more. Capital One Shopping

- **Online Shopping Frequency:** Men shop online more frequently than women. 24% of men shop online at least daily, compared to 17% of women. 70% of men shop online weekly. OnlineDasher

- **Information Preferences:** Men prefer objective information (make, model, speed, etc.) above subjective information, whereas women are more comprehensive and evaluate both objective and subjective aspects. The Times of India

- **Shopping Experience:** Women are more likely to experience problems while shopping than men — 53% vs. 48%, with women over age 40 reporting more issues. Knowledge at Wharton

- **Online Shopping Demographics:** The average online shopper is predominantly male, aged between 25 and 49 years. The interest rate of men buying online is 84.3%. SageSeller

- **E-Commerce Spending:** 84.3% of men buy online, compared with 77% of women. While women buy on average about 7.1 times a year, men buy less frequently but spend more per purchase. Adglow

- **Global Consumer Spending:** Women spend nearly $35 trillion globally on consumer goods, equivalent to 50% of worldwide consumer spending. FinanceBuzz

- **Diverging Shopping Habits:** Shopping habits amongst men and women are widening, with significant differences in preferences and behaviors. Charged Retail

- **In-Store Spending:** Men spend 75% more on goods bought in-store than women, indicating major differences in shopping habits by gender. Performance Marketing World

1.2.4 Psychological Techniques for Pricing: A Rush of Blood to the Head

"Too many companies want their brands to reflect some idealized, perfected image of themselves. As a consequence, their brands acquire no texture, no character."

– Richard Branson

You often evaluate prices by comparing them to others: past prices, competitors' prices, or even adjacent numbers. This 'reference price' in your brain plays a crucial role in how you perceive the value of a product. Motivation is taken from Nick Kolenda's Pricing Tactics'.

In this chapter of "Zero to Everyone," we delve into the art of pricing, not just to set a tag on your product but to skillfully play the symphony of the customer's mind. Buckle up as we navigate through visual tactics, framing techniques, numerical nuances, and the dynamics of discounts.

Visual Tactics: The Art of Perception

Ever noticed how prices in smaller fonts seem more… manageable? It's no coincidence. Smaller fonts make numerical values appear less daunting, subtly nudging customers towards a purchase. The positioning of prices also plays a crucial role. Placing them at the top or left taps into our visual processing biases, making them feel lighter and more affordable.

But it's not just about size and position. The typography of prices matters too. Removing commas (think ₹1200 vs. ₹1,200) and currency symbols lessens the 'pain' of parting with money. Clever use of alliteration – like "Five Dollar Footlong" – makes prices not only catchy but seemingly more reasonable. Red-colored prices, interestingly, often signal savings to men, a quirk that retailers can use to their advantage.

In emotional purchases, the focus shifts from price to experience. Here, the cost takes a backseat to the benefits and joys of the product.

Framing Techniques: Setting the Stage

How do you make a price seem smaller? Place it next to a larger number. This contrast creates a mental anchor, making the actual price more palatable. Sorting products from high to low sets a higher initial reference, and distinguishing expensive options establishes a premium benchmark, enhancing the appeal of mid-range products.

Daily equivalence framing – like "just $3 a day" – breaks down intimidating sums into digestible bites. However, beware of bundling cheap and expensive items together, as this can dilute perceived value. Transparency in pricing builds trust, and early budgeting can reduce the sting of spending. Refund strategies are also crucial; money returned is often spent more liberally.

Numerical Nuances: The Devil's in the Details

Ever wonder why ₹99 feels drastically cheaper than ₹100? It's all in the left digit. This small change can create a significant psychological gap. Prices with fewer syllables often seem cheaper, while breaking down prices into smaller units can make them appear more attractive. Precision in high prices suggests value, and tailored prices (think of numbers matching personal details like birthdays) add a personal touch.

For emotional or convenient purchases, round numbers work well. Small price differences in assortments simplify decision-making, and gradual price rises are less jarring. If you're operating in a price-sensitive market, consider downsizing features rather than the price itself.

Discount Dynamics: The Allure of Savings

Discounts need to scream attention. Visual distinction, spacing, and vertical placement enhance the perception of savings. Changing every digit in a discounted price (say from ₹50 to ₹35 instead of ₹50 to ₹34.99) can make the discount feel more substantial. For items below ₹100, percentage discounts often trump absolute amounts.

Interestingly, framing discounts as a rollback from a previous increase (like "was 25% higher") can be more enticing than straightforward discounts. This approach avoids setting a new, lower reference price in the customer's mind. Also, consider the timing and structure of your discounts. End-of-month discounts target budget-conscious customers, while tiered discounts create a ladder of attainable savings.

The effectiveness can vary based on context, culture, and your specific market. But wielded wisely, they can turn pricing from a mere number game into a strategic asset, driving sales and customer satisfaction.

As we conclude this chapter, reflect on how these techniques can be adapted to your unique marketing context. Pricing isn't just about covering costs and earning profits; it's a psychological journey, a rush of blood to the head, leading your customers from contemplation to exhilaration, all with a few cleverly placed numbers and cues.

In the next chapter, we'll explore how to build and nurture the emotional connection with your customers. Stay tuned, and let's continue this exciting journey from zero to everyone, one step at a time.

1.3 A Journey Through Maslow's Hierarchy of Needs

"Everything has beauty, but not everyone can see." – Confucius

Why do we do what we do?

Why do some things seem so vital to us, while others do not?

Well, sit back and let me take you on a little journey into the world of psychology, specifically through the lens of Abraham Maslow's famous theory - the Hierarchy of Needs.

Imagine you're building a pyramid (no, not in Egypt!). This pyramid is special; it's the pyramid of your life's needs and desires.

At the base of our pyramid, we have our **physiological needs**. Think about it – when you're really hungry, can you focus on anything else? These are our body's basic demands: food, water, and a nice, cozy bed to sleep in. Basically, everything we need to survive. When these are in short supply, nothing else seems to matter, right?

Once our stomachs are full and we're comfy in our homes, we move up a level to **safety needs**. Now, it's not just about surviving but also feeling secure. It's about having a safe place to live, knowing you won't lose your job tomorrow, and feeling healthy. It's that sigh of relief when you pay your insurance or when you know you're safe walking home at night.

Climbing up, we reach our **love and belonging needs**. This is where things get social! Humans are social creatures, and we crave connections. Friendships, family, and romantic relationships—these bonds are crucial. It's that warm, fuzzy feeling you get when surrounded by loved ones, or the joy in shared laughter. It's belonging to a community, whether it's your family at Thanksgiving or friends at a concert.

Next up, the **Esteem Needs**. This is all about respect and recognition. It's feeling valued and believing in your own worth. It's the pride in your accomplishments, the confidence when you ace an interview, and the respect you earn from peers. But remember, it's not just about getting respect from others; it's also about respecting yourself.

Finally, at the top of our pyramid is the **crown jewel**, Self-Actualization. This is the 'be all you can be' level. It's about fulfilling your potential, pursuing your passions, and realizing your dreams. It's those moments when you feel completely in tune with what you're doing, whether it's painting, solving a complex problem at work, or running a marathon. It's about becoming the best version of yourself.

Now, you might be thinking, "Do I need to complete one level to move on to the next?" Well, it's not a strict video game level-up system. Life is messy, and our needs don't always line up neatly. Sometimes we're juggling a few levels at once, or we might feel a need from a higher level even if a lower one isn't fully met. That's just being human!

Understanding this hierarchy is like having a map to our motivations. It helps us understand why we prioritize some things over others, why we feel what we feel, and why we strive for certain goals. It's a guide to understanding not just ourselves but also the people around us.

So, the next time you're feeling out of sorts or wondering why you're focusing on certain things, think about this pyramid. Where are you on it? What needs are you trying to fulfill? Remember, each level is important, and balancing them is key to a fulfilling life.

And that's Maslow's Hierarchy of Needs for you - a simple yet powerful tool for understanding our human motivations. It shows us that we're all on a journey, not just to meet our basic needs but to grow, connect, and ultimately find our own path to self-actualization.

1.4 Understanding Buyer Behavior

"Products are made in the factory, but brands are created in the mind."

– Walter Landor

Ready to dive into the fascinating world of what makes your customers tick, especially in the bustling markets of India? Let's unravel the mystery of consumer buyer behavior together.

Imagine you're at a bustling market in Mumbai or a busy shopping street in Delhi. Every person there makes decisions influenced by a mix of factors. We're talking about social, personal, psychological, and situational influences. Let's break them down in a way that makes sense for us in India.

Social Influences:

- **Culture:** Our rich Indian culture, with its diverse traditions and values, heavily influences our buying habits. Whether it's preferring certain foods, clothes, or technology, culture is a big player.

- **Social Class:** In India, the concept of social class can be complex. It's not just about wealth; it's about lifestyle, education, and even the kind of job you have.

Personal Influences:

Your age, job, income, and lifestyle—they all play a part. A young, tech-savvy professional in Bengaluru might look for the latest smartphone, while a retired person in Kolkata might prioritize health products.

Psychological Influences:

- **Motivation:** This is huge. Remember Maslow's hierarchy of needs? In India, it might start with basic needs like food and safety but then move up to social needs like belonging (think big fat Indian weddings!) and eventually to self-esteem and self-actualization.

- **Perception:** How we see a product can change based on our beliefs and attitudes. Maybe a family in Kerala perceives an electric car as a smarter choice due to environmental concerns.

- **Learning, beliefs, and attitudes:** Our experiences shape our choices. If a friend in Mumbai flaunts a new restaurant, you're likely to try it, right?

- **Freud and Maslow Theories:** Freud says that our purchases might be driven by deeper, unconscious desires. Maybe buying that luxury watch isn't just about telling time, but about the status it represents? Maslow, on the other hand, talks about fulfilling needs from basic to advanced, which marketers in India use to segment their audience.

Situational Influences:

The situation matters a lot. For instance, during festival seasons like Diwali or Eid, even the most budget-conscious shopper in India might splurge.

Understanding these factors is like having a roadmap in the minds of Indian consumers. Whether you're launching a new fashion label in Jaipur or opening a cafe in Goa, knowing what drives your customers can make all the difference.

So, there you have it—a snapshot of what influences buying behavior in the colorful, diverse world of Indian markets. Keep these in mind, and you'll be well on your way to marketing success!

1.5 Post-Purchase Cognitive Dissonance

"The consumer isn't a moron; she is your wife."

– David Ogilvy

Imagine you've just splurged on a high-end gadget. Initially, it felt like a rewarding purchase, but soon after, you start questioning your decision. Did you really need to spend that much? Could there have been a better, more economical option? This regret and second-guessing is a classic case of buyer's remorse.

OR... You buy a new smartphone, expecting lightning-fast performance and an exceptional camera, as advertised. However, the reality doesn't match up. The phone is sluggish, and the camera quality is mediocre. This gap between your expectations and the actual product performance leads to a sense of disappointment and frustration.

OR... You've just bought a trendy new outfit, feeling quite pleased with your choice. But then, your friends or family members express surprise or disapproval over your selection. Their reactions make you doubt your decision. Did you really make the right choice, or were you swayed by a passing trend?

OR... You're in the market for a new laptop. You research extensively, reading through countless reviews and comparing specs. But with so much information, making a decision becomes overwhelming. After the purchase, you're left wondering if you considered all the important factors or if you missed something crucial. This information overload can lead to uncertainty and doubt about your choice.

OR... After buying a new appliance, you stumble upon a series of negative reviews or hear about a friend's poor experience with the same model. This new information, encountered after your purchase, plants seeds of doubt. Did you make a mistake? Is the product really as good as you initially thought?

What is happening here?

When you embark on a journey to make a significant purchase, like a car or a high-end gadget, the stakes are naturally higher. The investment isn't just financial; it's emotional too. You expect this purchase to meet not only your needs but also to align with your aspirations. However, if reality falls short of your expectations, dissonance sets in. You start questioning your decision, wondering if you could have chosen better or if the investment was worth it at all.

Now, consider a situation where you're faced with ambiguity or uncertainty. You're looking to buy a product, but the information available is either scarce or conflicting. One review says it's excellent; another points out flaws. This lack of clarity can leave you in a state of doubt, questioning whether your decision to purchase is the right one. It's like trying to navigate a maze without a clear map.

Then there's the challenge of multiple attractive alternatives. You're in the market for a new smartphone, and every brand seems to offer something unique. One has a better camera, another boasts a longer battery life, and yet another is more budget-friendly. This abundance of choices, while seemingly beneficial, can actually lead to the fear of missing out. You might find yourself constantly wondering if the other option was better, leading to a lingering sense of dissatisfaction with your choice.

Cognitive overload is another hurdle you might face. In today's world, where information is abundant, making a decision can be overwhelming. When you're bombarded with too many choices and too much information, it becomes challenging to process it all effectively. This overload can lead to second-guessing your decisions as you wonder if you evaluated all options thoroughly.

Conflicting information can also lead to post-purchase dissonance. Imagine you buy a product based on certain advertised features, but post-purchase, you realize that the product doesn't quite live up to those promises. This discrepancy between what was promised and what is delivered can lead to a sense of betrayal and dissatisfaction.

In each of these scenarios, the common thread is the psychological conflict you experience after making a purchase. This dissonance is not just about the product or service itself; it's about how well your expectations align with reality and how external factors influence your perception of your purchase. Understanding these dynamics is crucial for both consumers and businesses, as it helps in making more informed decisions and creating strategies that enhance customer satisfaction.

Strategies to Reduce Post-Purchase Dissonance

- **Accurate Product Information:** Provide clear, detailed, and honest information about your products. This transparency helps set realistic expectations.

- **Realistic Expectation Setting:** Avoid over-promising in your marketing. Be honest about what your product can and cannot do.

- **Customer Reviews and Testimonials**: Display genuine customer feedback. This not only builds trust but also gives prospective buyers a realistic idea of what to expect.

- **Responsive Customer Support:** Offer multiple channels for support and address customer concerns promptly and effectively.

- **Hassle-Free Return Policy:** A straightforward return policy reassures customers that they can return a product if it doesn't meet their expectations.

- **Post-Purchase Communication:** Follow up with customers after their purchase. This shows that you care about their experience and are willing to support them.

Benefits of Reducing Post-Purchase Dissonance for Customers:

- **Increased Satisfaction:** Aligning expectations with reality enhances the shopping experience.

- **Enhanced Confidence:** Customers feel more confident in their decision-making abilities.

- **Improved Well-Being:** Reducing dissonance alleviates negative emotions like regret and anxiety.

- **Time and Effort Savings:** A satisfying purchase experience saves customers the hassle of dealing with returns or exchanges.

- **Trust and Loyalty:** Efforts to minimize dissonance foster customer loyalty and trust.

In conclusion, post-purchase cognitive dissonance is a critical aspect of the customer experience that can significantly impact your business. By understanding its causes and implementing strategies to reduce it, you can enhance customer satisfaction, foster loyalty, and build a strong, reputable brand. Remember, a satisfied customer is not just a repeat buyer but also a valuable advocate for your business. So, take proactive steps to ensure your customers feel confident and happy with their purchases, and watch your business grow from zero to everyone.

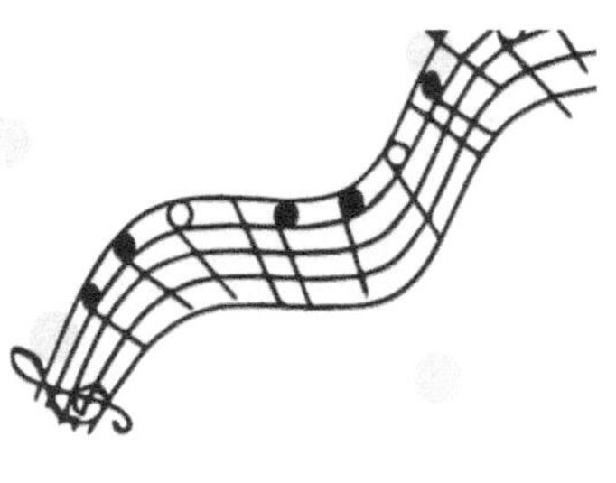

BrANdING

2. Branding

2.1 I Am Not A Company

"Your brand is a story unfolding across all customer touch points."

– Jonah Sachs

There is a reason for this, because most of the companies are getting confused because they think that is their Brand Name.

One of the common mistakes you make is making your consumers confused by putting the company name in front of them.

But what you actually do is endorse your brand name.

This "company name" is like "publisher of the book" but actually you buy it because of the "author or idea".

So who will you focus on?

Yes, you got it right... You need your full focus on the BRAND NAME.

Before I give your brain a hit with knowledge, let's clear up some of the basics here. Just be with me while I curse you with knowledge.

A **company name is the legal name** under which a business entity operates and is registered. It is the official name that appears on legal documents such as contracts, licenses, and tax filings. **It identifies the legal entity that owns and operates the business and is often chosen to reflect the nature of the company's business or its founders.**

On the other hand, **a "brand name" is a name, term, design, symbol,** or any other feature that identifies a product or service of a company and distinguishes it from its competitors. **A brand name is typically used for marketing and advertising purposes to create a unique identity for a company's products or services.**

While a company name and brand name may be the same, they often differ because a company may have multiple brands under its umbrella. For example, Procter & Gamble is a company name that owns several brands, such as Tide, Crest, and Gillette.

With this caveat in mind, a company name is a company name as long as the name is not being used as a brand. And a Brand is a Brand. There is a clear-cut difference.

I am a fan of the **JIO network, and** I know you might be too. The way they have reduced the price, it is nearly impossible to get data at such a cheap rate in India.

Now that we have it, why not take their example to explain to you how to focus deeply on branding? Also, I always save the best information so that you need to go through what I am trying to explain.

Company Name: Reliance Industries Limited

Brand Name: Jio

Reliance Industries Limited (RIL) is the legal name of the company and is a conglomerate that operates in various industries such as oil and gas, petrochemicals, and telecommunications. Jio is a brand under RIL that provides telecommunications services.

Confusing RIL with Jio can lead to brand identity confusion and legal issues if another company owns the trademark for the Jio brand name.

It can also make it difficult for RIL to expand its product offerings under different brand names. Therefore, it's important for RIL to maintain clear distinctions between its brand names and company names to avoid these issues and maintain a strong brand identity.

Very powerful thing was said above about expansion. Every owner needs to understand that if they promote their company. They are killing their chances of expansion. If managers of companies understand that products sell because of brands in consumers' minds.

The common issues that businesses may face when their company name is confused with their brand name:

Brand Dilution:

When customers are confused about a company's brand name, it can lead to a lack of brand recognition and dilute the brand's value. This can result in decreased customer loyalty and lost sales.

Trademark Infringement:

If a company's brand name is confused with its company name, it can lead to legal issues if another business already owns the trademark for that brand name. This can lead to costly legal battles, a potential loss of brand equity, and brand name changes.

Marketing Challenges:

Confusing a company name with a brand name can make it challenging for businesses to develop effective marketing strategies. It can also make it difficult to track and measure the effectiveness of marketing efforts.

Limited Product Offerings:

If a company's brand name is confused with its company name, it can limit its ability to expand its product or service offerings under different brand names. This can hinder the company's ability to diversify its revenue streams and grow its business.

Brand Reputation Damage:

Confusing a company name with a brand name can damage a company's brand reputation. If customers associate a poor experience with a particular brand, it can negatively impact the overall reputation of the company.

Most of the issues involving company names versus brand names can be solved by asking yourself these questions. By the way, these were described by Al Ries.

1. What is the name of the BRAND?

2. What is the name of the stuff inside the packaging?

2.2 How do Luxury Brands Weave this Enchanting Narrative?

"A brand is no longer what we tell the consumer it is – it is what consumers tell each other it is."

– Scott Cook

Man 1: Come on Man!! Why this T-shirt? It does not look good and price is still high.

Man 2: Bro this is "ZORO" brand… It is perfect.

Man 1: I don't see this any good product.

Man 2: Nah, I am going to BUY it.

Now you see right where the GAP in buying. The person is going to buy LUXURY whether or not it is a great product or now. I know you are more than excited to know how luxury is created in our mind.

Let's delve into the "how." How do luxury brands weave this enchanting narrative?

And more intriguingly, how can you, as a storyteller, brand creator, or marketer, replicate this alchemy of allure?

Step 1: Crafting the Status Signal

Tanishq, one of India's premier jewelry brands, often uses celebrity endorsements in its advertising campaigns. A recent example includes their association with Deepika Padukone, a renowned Bollywood actress. These endorsements elevate the brand's status, associating it with luxury, elegance, and sophistication.

Consider the status signal your brand emits. For instance, if you're designing a luxury brand, your product must symbolize something beyond its functional value. It should whisper tales of exclusivity and prestige. How? By associating with symbols of status: perhaps an endorsement by a renowned figure or by presenting your product in settings synonymous with luxury and power.

Step 2: Mastering the Art of Distance

You might know......

Sabyasachi's bridal wear collections are often showcased in grand settings, with models photographed in luxurious, palatial environments. This creates a sense of exclusivity and unattainability, positioning the brand in a dream-like, aspirational world.

Creating a sense of distance is crucial. This doesn't mean making your product inaccessible, but rather cultivating an aura of exclusivity. Use imagery that positions your product just beyond the reach of the average person. Think of high-end fashion ads: the models and products often appear in surreal or grandiose settings, hinting at a world that's elevated from the ordinary.

Step 3: Embracing the Cold Touch

Oh yes, The Oberoi's…

The Oberoi Hotels are known for their impeccable service that strikes a balance between warmth and professionalism. Their customer interaction is reserved yet attentive, creating a luxury experience that feels exclusive and prestigious.

The 'cold touch' is about the brand's interaction with its audience. Luxury brands often maintain a reserved, almost aloof demeanor. In your communications, whether it's social media, advertising, or in-store experience, balance warmth with a hint of detachment. This fine line creates an allure, making customers seek approval from the brand.

Step 4: Narrating the Craftsmanship Tale

We all love Fashion Brands and how you make it a LUXURY…

Anita Dongre's fashion brand stands out for its emphasis on craftsmanship and sustainability. The brand often shares stories about its grassroots approach, highlighting the artisans' skills and the meticulous handiwork that goes into each piece, connecting customers with the brand's heritage and ethical values.

The story of craftsmanship is where emotion weaves into the fabric of your brand. Share the tales behind your product's creation—the artisans, the meticulous process, the rare materials. This storytelling transforms your product from a mere item to a piece of heritage, imbuing it with deeper value and meaning.

Step 5: Implementing the Minimalist Mystique

Aha…… Now you tell me if you have not dreamt of going for stay in LEELA PALACE

The Leela's properties often feature minimalist yet opulent designs. Their use of space, both in architecture and interior decor, exudes a sense of luxury and exclusivity, making each property feel like a tranquil oasis away from the bustle of the city.

Minimalism in luxury branding isn't just about aesthetics; it's about focus. In a world cluttered with information and products, minimalism allows your luxury brand to stand out as a beacon of calm and assurance. Utilize space, both physical and visual, to highlight the exclusivity and rarity of your product.

Step 6: Making the Bold Statement

This man is too famous to stitch OUR clothes……

Manish Malhotra is known for his bold and innovative designs in Indian fashion. He often challenges traditional aesthetics with his modern take on ethnic wear. This boldness sets his brand apart, making it synonymous with contemporary luxury.

Lastly, don't fear boldness. Luxury brands often break norms and challenge conventional aesthetics. Embrace designs or strategies that set you apart, even if they seem unconventional. Remember, luxury is as much about individuality as it is about quality.

> **"If people believe they share values with a company, they will stay loyal to the brand."**
>
> **– Howard Schultz**

I like to love things.

I like to have anger issues

I like to admire people

I like to learn quality things

I like to help someone in need

I like to taste good food

I like to look good.

For sure, you also have the same needs as I do. But this need, as a general factor is not taken into account when I see people trying to create their brands. Yes, one of the common human tendencies is to look into credentials. Let's say you want to hire someone in your company. What is the first thing you look at in his or her qualifications? Until you are okay with the person's experience or ability to do things, well, that rarely happens

The same is true when you are building a brand. Don't think that you are going to create a presence in front of humans just by putting your product there and thinking people will come to you because you are just a good product. People often look at your authenticity or the testimonials that make up your credentials.

The important piece is **"sense of belonging."**

When I say I have an iPhone, it implies that I belong to a sophisticated group. Or if I say that I drink Coca-Cola, that means I am young and full of energy. Does your brand sound like a place where you want them to belong? Or you are just letting them go with your product and not making them recurring. (More on publicity later; now let's clear basics first.)

You should **fall in love with your customers.** Only then can you discover what they need and where you can position your product. Falling in love with your customers and building a brand that they love and want to be a part of is an important aspect of creating a successful and sustainable business.

In the case of building a voice, **you should always look into the story your customers are listening to**. Yeah, you tell a lot of stories, but what they are listening to might be completely different. Develop a clear and compelling brand identity that aligns with your customers' values and resonates with them. Create a strong brand voice and visual identity, and be consistent in your messaging and marketing efforts.

I will give a few points that kind of make your steps to work easier…

Creating a great movie often involves a blend of key elements that contribute to its narrative appeal and ability to captivate audiences. So here I am presenting the Unified Outline for Great Movies and Brand Narratives:

1. **Introduction (Engaging Hook)**

   Movie Narrative: It starts with a scene that immediately captivates the audience, like an intense situation or a mysterious character.

   Brand Story: Begins by highlighting a unique aspect of the brand or addressing a specific consumer need.

2. **Protagonist (Character with a Problem)**

   Movie Narrative: Introduces a relatable protagonist who faces a significant conflict or challenge.

   Brand Story: The customer is the protagonist, facing a problem or need that the brand can address.

3. **Mentor/Guide**

   Movie Narrative: A mentor figure appears to provide guidance and support to the protagonist.

   Brand Story: The brand positions itself as a guide, offering expertise, reassurance, and solutions.

4. **Plan (Guide Offers a Solution)**

   Movie Narrative: The mentor provides a plan or strategy for the protagonist to overcome their challenges.

   Brand Story: The brand presents its products or services as the solution to the customer's problem.

5. **Call to Action**

   Movie Narrative: The protagonist is compelled to take action, following the mentor's plan.

   Brand Story: Customers are encouraged to engage with the brand, using its products or services.

6. **Avoiding Failure**

   Movie Narrative: The protagonist navigates challenges and obstacles, using the plan to avoid failure.

   Brand Story: The brand demonstrates how its solutions help customers avoid negative outcomes.

7. **Climax and Resolution**

   Movie Narrative: The story reaches a climax with the protagonist overcoming their main conflict, leading to a resolution.

   Brand Story: The brand story showcases the success and transformation achieved by customers using its products or services.

8. **Transformation and Success**

   Movie Narrative: The protagonist experiences growth and transformation, achieving success.

   Brand Story: The brand narrative highlights how customers achieve success and transformation through their products/services.

9. **Emotional Connection**

   Movie Narrative: The story creates a deep emotional bond with the audience, making them invested in the protagonist's journey.

Brand Story: The brand establishes an emotional connection with customers, making them feel part of the brand's journey.

10. **Incorporating Universal Themes**

   Movie Narrative: Themes like courage, love, or perseverance are woven into the story.

   Brand Story: The brand integrates universal themes that resonate with its audience, like empowerment, innovation, or community.

11. **Memorable Conclusion**

   Movie Narrative: Ends with a powerful, memorable scene that leaves a lasting impact.

   Brand Story: Concludes with a strong message or vision, reinforcing the brand's impact and leaving a lasting impression on the customer.

12. **World-building (If Applicable)**

   Movie Narrative: In genres like fantasy or sci-fi, detailed world-building enhances the story.

   Brand Story: The brand develops a unique identity and culture, creating an immersive experience for customers.

How about that? Let's move on to next awesome chapter.

2.3 At the Back of My Mind

"Branding is the art of becoming knowable, likable, and trustable."

– John Jantsch

This topic can be a **little controversial…**

Why?

Because what I am going to give is the **advantage of working the brain.** And how you can utilize this to make an effective presence. This definitely should be utilized by CEOs who are afraid to begin. I would say, **DON'T WORRY and just have FAITH…**

Do you know how our brain makes decisions? I think you do now… but I will just recap a little bit here too

Our brain **first receives information from our senses** (e.g., what we see, hear, or feel) about the situation we're in. Then, our brain evaluates this information based on our current goals, needs, and preferences. This evaluation helps our brain determine what options we have and what outcomes we can expect from each option.

Next, our brain integrates all of this information to **weigh the pros and cons of each option**. Once the brain has weighed the options, it makes a decision and **sends signals to our muscles** to act on that decision.

Finally, **our brain receives feedback from the action we took**, and it uses this feedback to update its evaluation and decision-making processes for future situations.

Imagine you are driving and see a billboard about "Breaking Bad." Now that we are so emotionally attached to the series, we would like to know more. So these advertisements have a definite Call-To- Action. That is how everyone can manipulate their decision making. These advertisements invoke emotions and fit a pattern in the mind.

To what extent emotions are rational…

Incidental emotions can influence people's judgments and evaluations of neutral stimuli, such as consumer products, political candidates, or other stimuli encountered in daily life. People tend to misattribute their emotional state to the target object, **leading them to overvalue or undervalue the object based on the emotions they are experiencing.**

The role of culture in shaping emotional experiences and expressions, as well as the potential for emotional intelligence training to improve emotional regulation and decision-making skills.

The role of various neurotransmitters, including dopamine and serotonin, in modulating emotional and cognitive processes.

Emotions are not irrational, but rather serve as important signals that can guide our decision-making in rational ways. Emotions can be seen as a form of data processing, providing us with information about the world around us and our own experiences.

Emotions can help us make more efficient and effective decisions, particularly in situations where there is limited information or time for analysis.

You are aware of how the brain makes decisions. We are constantly making unconscious, emotion based decisions. **According to study, 30-60 percent of decisions we make, we don't we know why we made them. We did it emotionally and justified it with logic.**

Hmm, Emotional Buying…

A person feeling very scared is going to have a spike in adrenaline.

A person who feels secure and comfortable will have dopamine and serotonin.

When people are in a positive mood, they are more likely to make impulsive and emotional purchases. They may be more willing to spend money and less concerned about the consequences of their purchases. Positive moods can also lead to a greater focus on the benefits of a product rather than its costs.

In contrast, when people are in a negative mood, they may be more inclined to make emotional purchases as a way of regulating their emotions.

For example, they may buy comfort food or a luxury item to help them feel better. Negative moods can also lead to greater attention to product details and prices, as individuals may be looking for a distraction or a way to feel in control.

When people are in a neutral mood, their emotional buying behavior may be influenced by a variety of factors, such as social norms, cultural values, and individual personality traits.

For example, some individuals may be more impulsive and likely to make emotional purchases regardless of their mood, while others may be more cautious and rational in their decision-making.

A brand needs to keep drawing attention because of the emotions associated with it.

When I was a kid, my father used to drop me off at school on his Scooter…

Well, this is the strategy called Nostalgia. Nostalgia can play a significant role in brand building and sales. **Past experience impacts future decision making.** A positive experience will yield positive results.

Nostalgia is a powerful emotion that can create a **strong emotional connection between consumers and brands**. Brands that are associated with positive memories from the past can evoke feelings of warmth, comfort, and familiarity, which can lead to increased brand loyalty and repeat purchases.

In a crowded marketplace, by tapping into consumers' memories and emotions, brands can differentiate themselves and create a sense of authenticity and credibility.

Bajaj Chetak was a popular scooter brand in India that was manufactured by Bajaj Auto from 1972 to 2006. In 2020, the brand was relaunched as an electric scooter, **evoking a sense of nostalgia among Indian consumers who grew up with the iconic two-wheeler.**

The relaunch campaign featured a series of ads that paid tribute to the brand's legacy and its iconic design. The ads highlighted the features and benefits of the new electric scooter while tapping into the emotional connection that Indians had with the original Bajaj Chetak.

The campaign was a huge success, generating a lot of buzz on social media and winning several awards for its creativity and effectiveness. By using **nostalgia as a marketing tool, Bajaj Auto was able to create a unique brand** identity and differentiate itself from its competitors in the electric scooter market.

Our brain wants to choose one option quicker than the other. **As individuals, we are the actors in our story**. So when someone steps in our memory lane, it reminds us of previous times we **made the same successful decisions.**

When time is low, emotion drives choices…… so is with time is high, and choices are high

Research says that when the time allowed for a decision is short, automatic emotions are likely to drive choices. When time allowed is high and exposure to choices is high, the desirable outcome will again be selected.

When time allowed is high and exposure to choices is low, we are less likely to buy with emotions.

Very strong BRANDS and powerful POLITICAL leaders become habits for many…

Habits are largely insensitive to change.

Goals contribute to habit formation by increasing attention. Goals provide a means for cueing and strengthening habit formation. **A brand can take actions that get a customer to repeat a behavior that would create desired habits.**

People tend to develop habits based on their experiences and the positive or negative **associations they have with certain behaviors, products, or personalities**. When a brand or a political leader consistently delivers positive experiences or messages that align with a person's values and beliefs, that person is more likely to develop the habit of using or supporting that brand or leader.

For example, a person who grew up drinking Coca-Cola may develop the habit of choosing Coke over other soft drinks because they associate it with positive memories and experiences. Similarly, a person who strongly identifies with the political ideology and message of a particular leader may develop the **habit of voting for that leader or supporting their policies.**

The power of habits is that they can be difficult to break, even if a person's circumstances or preferences change. Therefore, brands and political leaders that are able to establish strong **habits among their audience are more likely to enjoy long-term success and loyalty.**

2.4 Assets & Liabilities

"Your brand is what other people say about you when you're not in the room."

– Jeff Bezos

Do you remember the "You press the button, we do the rest" campaign?

Well, don't stress; nobody does now.

Even I was confused when I learned about it. And moreover, I was surprised to know it was from KODAK.

We knew Kodak as an innovator in the photography industry. Indeed, it was once a dominant player. I think it was so ICONIC to have a Kodak camera at home.

I recall when my grandfather bought it and clicked the first photo of me. Now I think it was such an emotional gesture.

As the century turned, so did the Kodak brand. Kodak struggled to adapt to the changing landscape. However, as the industry evolved with the advent of digital photography.

Even for a long time, you might also remember that Kodak used traditional films. It is also very hard to change. This lack of innovation, coupled with a weak brand identity, led to Kodak's decline and eventual bankruptcy in 2012.

A company that was stuck in the past

They failed to adapt to changing consumer needs and preferences. And it did not invest enough in its brand identity to stay relevant in the digital age.

Have you ever wondered about BRAND EQUITY?

I have the simplest explanation, **it is a set of assets and liabilities linked to a brand's name**. Major categories given by famous David Aaker:

1. Brand name awareness
2. Brand loyalty
3. Perceived Quality
4. Brand associations

Assets and Liabilities will be affected and even lost if the band name or symbols changes. There might be chances some might be shifted to the new name and symbols.

Let's accumulate assets. You want it, right?

Asset 1: Awareness

"Top of the Mind is equal to **Tip of the Tongue"**

This refers to the strength of the brand's presence in the consumer's mind. Well, it can also be developed through repeated billboards.

Research shows that recognition alone can result in more positive feelings towards anything. Let's take an example of music you are listening to, people you work with daily, or even brands. So it makes sense that a familiar brand will always have an edge.

Asset 2: Perceived Quality

"Brand is a Battle Ship"

Perceived quality is a brand association that is elevated to the status of a brand asset:

- It drives financial performance

- The strategic thrust of a business

- Aspects how brand is looked

Quality is usually at the heart of what customers are buying. It is a measure of brand identity. Studies show that **perceptions of "goodness" are closely related to quality.** When QUALITY improves, so generally do other elements of customers' perceptions of the brand.

A brand is like a ship facing an upcoming battle. Other sub-brands, like other ships, need to be coordinated. Our Big Enemy is our competitor; they know our location and strengths. The perceptions and motivations of customers will work as winds. When the wind is in our favor, we win.

Asset 3: Loyalty

"Your brand is what other people say about you when you're not in the room."

Highly loyal customer base is expected to generate a very predictable sales and profit stream. In fact, a brand without a loyal customer base is usually vulnerable. They are eventually going to blow up when storms arrive.

Do not make a mistake to entice customers!!

You can enhance loyalty for the customers who are on the fence. This means they are not able to differentiate between two brands. I know you want know what next thing you can do:

1. **Frequent Buyer Program:** This will provide direct reinforcement for loyal behavior. Like rebates from credit for spending certain limits.

2. **Customer Clubs:** Kids who joined Nintendo Fun Club were at the heart of early access to new games. Club members receive discounts, upcoming events and special offers.

3. **Database Marketing:** Data of customers can be used for marketing at narrowed segments. Tailored customers will feel that the brand is connecting to them individually.

Bang!! You've got your loyal customer there. Happy 😬

Asset 4: Associations

How your customers associate brands with each other plays a great part. It totally depends on how you want to set up in Customer's mind.

A key to building a strong brand is developing an identity.

Customers may associate certain values, emotions, or experiences with them. For example, a luxury fashion brand may be associated with exclusivity, sophistication

FabIndia - Customers may associate FabIndia with sustainable and ethically-sourced clothing and home goods, as the company places a strong emphasis on supporting local artisans and using natural materials.

2.5 Promote Your Category (P - Y - C)

"If people believe they share values with a company, they will stay loyal to the brand."

– Howard Schultz

What I meant in the headline was "Promote Your Category.". The idea behind this is that rather than focusing solely on promoting your brand, you should promote the overall category or industry in which the brand operates.

Many will not agree with me on this because they will think that they are cutting their stomachs. But this is what you need to do to change the mindset. Think with an abundance mindset. If you promote the category, it is going to increase the size of the pie rather than slice it.

For example, if a leading brand of yogurt wants to increase sales, instead of solely promoting their brand of yogurt, they could focus on promoting the benefits of eating yogurt in general, such as its health benefits or versatility in recipes. By doing so, they are not only promoting their own brand but also creating a larger demand for yogurt as a category, which benefits the industry as a whole.

Promoting the category rather than just the brand can also help increase consumer awareness and understanding of the benefits of the product or service. It can also help to differentiate the product from its competitors and increase the perceived value of the product or service, which can lead to increased sales and customer loyalty.

What happens if you contract that much? It does not have any categories. Then I would suggest creating one. You will think what a psycho I am. I'm saying something out of order here. But believe me, creating a category is more profitable than you think.

Before Domino's created a 30 min delivery, was there any such category? I think not. Now everyone wants pizza in 30 minutes. This is what happens when you create one. Also, it makes you a leader in that. We humans like to know who came first, and by default, we see them as leaders.

As said by Al Ries and Laura Ries, "branding is perceived as capturing a bigger market share of an existing market. But the most efficient and useful aspect has nothing to do with market share. It is in creating a new category.".

Bear Grylls is not only known for promoting the categories of adventure and survival but also for creating a new category that has helped in building his brand. Through his unique approach to survival and adventure, Bear Grylls has created a new category of extreme survival that has captivated audiences around the world.

By pushing the boundaries of what was previously thought possible in terms of survival and adventure, Bear Grylls has created a new category that combines extreme sports, survival skills, and exploration. This new category has given rise to a new market for products and services related to extreme survival, such as survival gear, training programs, and adventure tourism.

Through his TV shows, books, and other media, Bear Grylls has promoted this new category and built a brand around it. His approach to extreme survival has become a hallmark of his brand and has helped to differentiate him from other adventure and survival experts.

Bear Grylls has also leveraged his brand to create a range of products and services that cater to this new category, including survival gear, outdoor clothing, and adventure tours. By creating a new category and building his brand around it, Bear Grylls has been able to expand his reach and impact, inspiring millions of people around the world to explore their limits and push themselves beyond their comfort zones.

To create a brand in a non-existing category or to make something out of nothing, you have to do these things:

1. Launch your brand in such a way to create a perception that your brand was first, the original.

2. Promote Your Category

Now you might be wondering why this will work. I have got that covered below:

1. When a brand promotes the category instead of just itself, it **focuses on the benefits** of the product or service as a whole, rather than just its own features.

2. This approach creates a **sense of trust and authority** for the brand because customers see it as an expert in the field.

3. It also creates a **sense of community** around the product or service, as customers who share a common interest are more likely to connect with one another.

4. By promoting the category, the brand can **differentiate itself from its competitors** and stand out in a crowded marketplace.

5. This approach can also **create more demand for the product or service**, not just for the brand promoting it but for the entire category as a whole.

6. By focusing on the category, the brand can create **a long-term relationship** with its customers by establishing itself as a trusted partner in the field.

7. This strategy can help **build customer loyalty and repeat business** because customers feel connected to the brand and the larger category it represents.

8. It can also help **increase the perceived value of the product or service**, leading to increased sales and customer satisfaction.

9. Promoting the category instead of just the brand can be especially **effective for new or niche products** or services that are not well-known in the market.

10. Ultimately, this approach is about **creating a bigger picture for the customer**, helping them see the benefits of the product or service beyond just what one brand can offer.

When you are first, you can dominate the category. You are the only brand associated with the concept. You have a powerful publicity platform. You need to put your money behind the concept itself, so the concept will take off, pulling the brand with it.

2.6 Identifying Uniqueness to Differentiate

"Branding is about signals – the signals people use to determine what you stand for as a brand. Signals create associations."

– Allen P. Adamson

As a person we distinguish each other by names. BUT these are not only things we look into. We do ask questions like:

What are my CORE values?

What do I STAND for?

How I want to be PERCEIVED?

What personality traits do I want to project?

What are important RELATIONSHIPS in my life?

To uniquely identify a person, you need to understand many aspects. Similarly, it is with the BRANDs. They too have an identity, which is used to make them stand out from the crowd. To create an impactful brand, you need to treat it like your BABY.

From naming to giving values, it is what BRAND wants......

Before I give you the points to think about, let me tell you what deceptions can create ineffectiveness in your strategies:

1. **Image Trap:**

   If you let customers dictate who you are, it is going to be a problem. It might not be the message they are spreading. Creating an identity is more than finding out what customers say they want.

   A BRAND IDENTITY should not accept existing perceptions but instead be willing to create changes.

2. **Position Trap:**

   A position is the USP of the Brand. That means its value proposition is actively communicated to the target audience.

   It becomes a trap when the search for brand identity becomes a search for position. It stops the growth of the BRAND. So many strategists have to throw out the messaging that creates such nuances.

   Let's again take the example of India's great BRAND Amul. An Indian dairy cooperative is an iconic brand known for its diverse range of dairy products. Established in 1946, it has become synonymous with quality, affordability, and trustworthiness.

Amul as a Product:

Amul offers a wide range of dairy products, including milk, butter, cheese, ice cream, yogurt, and more. The brand focuses on maintaining high-quality standards, ensuring freshness, and offering affordable pricing. Amul's diverse product line caters to various customer segments, from daily household consumption to professional industries like hotels and restaurants. Amul's consistent product quality and innovation have helped establish it as a market leader in the Indian dairy sector.

Amul as an Organization:

Amul operates as a cooperative model, owned by millions of farmers and managed by the Gujarat Cooperative Milk Marketing Federation (GCMMF). This unique structure emphasizes the brand's commitment to empowering farmers, providing fair prices, and promoting a sense of community. Amul's organizational structure and values have played a significant role in shaping its brand identity as a socially responsible and ethically-driven entity.

Amul as a Person:

Amul's brand personality is often seen as approachable, friendly, and trustworthy. The brand's long-standing advertising campaign, featuring the Amul girl, has humanized the brand through witty, humorous, and topical ads that resonate with Indian consumers. Amul's consistent tone of voice, relatability, and focus on Indian values and culture have helped create a strong emotional connection with its audience.

Amul as a Symbol:

Amul's logo and the Amul girl mascot have become iconic symbols representing the brand. The logo, featuring a red-and-white color scheme and a custom typeface, is easily recognizable and reflects the brand's commitment to quality, purity, and trust. The Amul girl, a hand-drawn character introduced in 1967, has become an integral part of the brand's identity, symbolizing innocence, wit, and the brand's close relationship with its customers.

"A brand vision should attempt to go beyond functional benefits to consider organizational values; a higher purpose; brand personality; and emotional, social, and self-expressive benefits."

– David Aaker

David A. Aaker, a renowned marketing expert and author, developed a brand identity framework known as the "Aaker Model." This model consists of four key pillars that are crucial for building strong brands. These pillars are:

Brand as a Product:

In this pillar, the focus is on the **product attributes, quality, features, and the value it delivers to customers.** The product's role in the market, the target audience, and its relationship with other products in the portfolio are also essential factors. A successful brand provides a unique value proposition, differentiates itself from competitors, and consistently delivers on its promises.

Like Visa, it is known for Credit Cards

It also relates to the association with the product. Its association with:

- Use Occasion *[Sure, Excel is used for cleaning clothes as well as occasionally disinfecting a variety of things.]*

- Users *[Nike offers sportswear, while Blackberry offers Corporate Wears]*

The country of origin also plays a role in recognizing a good product. Japanese made technology is more famous around the world than Japanese food.

Brand as an Organization:

The organization behind the brand is vital in shaping its identity. **This pillar focuses on the company's values, culture, mission, and vision, which contribute to the brand's overall image**.

Your brand should reflect the organization's core values and leverage its unique strengths to create a distinct identity. Consumers often associate the brand with the company's reputation, which can influence their perception and trust.

Competitors can copy product attributes, but **not Organizational Attributes.**

Brand as a Person:

This pillar is about the brand's **personality, tone of voice, and emotional associations.** Brands can be seen as having human-like characteristics, which can help create an emotional connection with customers.

A brand's personality should be authentic, consistent, and relatable to the target audience. It helps differentiate the brand from its competitors and **fosters a deeper, more meaningful relationship with customers.**

Example: Apple users identify themselves as casual, anti-corporate and creative.

Brand as a Symbol:

Symbols play a significant role in representing and communicating the essence of a brand. This pillar focuses on the visual elements of the brand, such as the logo, color palette, typography, and other design elements that make it recognizable and memorable.

Additionally, this can include mascots or other symbolic elements that evoke specific emotions or associations. A strong brand leverages visual symbols to create a lasting impression and evoke the desired emotional response in its target audience.

No good example I can think of aside from Nike's "Swoosh"

By considering each pillar, businesses can develop a cohesive and compelling brand strategy that resonates with their target audience, differentiates them from competitors, and fosters long-term customer loyalty.

Now you know how you can create your BRAND IDENTITY.

By using these strategies, you are giving soul to your brand. When you develop something with fundamental correctness and values, it is bound to grow.

2.6 Create a Word You Should Own

"Your personal brand is a promise to your clients… a promise of quality, consistency, competency, and reliability."

– Jason Hartman

You want to buy a Mercedes, not because of its good features. But I would say you want to buy because of the prestige you want to show in your community. This one word resonates with Mercedes so much that you know this from the heart. Your mind has been trained regularly by their advertisements and marketing.

Can you do the same for your brand? Let's pick up some other examples too:

Nike: "Just Do It"

Apple: "Innovative" or "Sleek"

Coca-Cola: "Refreshment" or "Happiness"

McDonald's: "Fast" or "Convenient"

Google: "Search" or "Knowledge"

Amazon: "Convenience" or "Selection"

BMW: "Luxury" or "Performance"

Samsung: "Innovation" or "Technology"

Pepsi: "Refreshing" or "Cool"

Toyota: "Reliability" or "Efficiency"

Words are key to unlock the potential of your brand

– Akash Jaiswal

You definitely connect with the brand through words. But here you might be confused then why should brands spend on color, shapes, and sizes? If I say, "Close your eyes and let someone say a few words in sequence, like NASA, astronaut, space, moon, dog. What have you imagined? You might have imagined a dog in a spacesuit on the moon. Isn't it amazing? How our mind works We, without even noticing, are trapped in our minds' pictorial imagination.

Our mind creates visual reality by using words. Only when the mind thinks that an object is large or small, beautiful or ugly, dark or light, does that meaning arise. But you need to understand that you need to reduce the essence of your brand to a single thought. This thought should be associated with a single attribute, and this attribute should be owned by no one.

A word that nobody owns

With the advancement of AI like ChatGPT, the process of refining and defining your brand has become streamlined. You yourself can engage in the process of building something out of a box. As an example, you can make use of AI and ask questions like, "Consider yourself a T-shirt company owner, and your target market is kids. T shirts are made of cotton for kids' comfort. Can you give me one word that will resonate and be unique for my company?"

You will be shocked by the response I got:

"Playful"

This word suggests that your T-shirts are not just comfortable but also fun and enjoyable for kids to wear. It can also imply that your T-shirts feature designs or patterns that are bright, colorful, and imaginative, appealing to children's sense of creativity and playfulness. Using this word in your brand messaging and marketing efforts can help position your T-shirt company as a playful and enjoyable option for kids and their parents.

If you weren't first in a category,

You can create a new category by simply narrowing your focus

So once your brand starts to grow, don't go and start expanding your brand. Because you will start ruining your word where you have already begun. Here's what you should do, expand the market, not the brand. It will help you grow exponentially. As an example, you know that Mercedes built the market for expensive cars by using a prestige strategy. Lamborghinis are expensive, but they do not convey the prestige of Mercedes.

The Indian motorcycle brand Royal Enfield has successfully used the word **"Bullet"** as a way to position itself as a rugged, powerful, and adventurous brand. The word "bullet" has become synonymous with the Royal Enfield brand in India and is often used interchangeably with the name of the motorcycle itself.

Royal Enfield has been manufacturing motorcycles since 1901, and the Bullet model has been in production since the 1940s. Over the years, the Bullet has become an iconic brand in India, associated with a sense of freedom, adventure, and individuality.

By using the word **"bullet"** as its brand positioning, Royal Enfield has been able to tap into this sense of adventure and individuality, resonating with its target audience of motorcycle enthusiasts and adventure seekers. The brand has also been able to differentiate itself from other motorcycle brands in India, which often focus on speed or affordability.

The success of Royal Enfield's brand positioning strategy can be seen in its strong brand loyalty among Indian consumers and its growing popularity in international markets.

This is applicable in all different categories, no matter how narrow or obscure the industry. Now you should try to determine how large a market your brand can acquire by narrowing its focus and owning a word.

Hola!!!

That was amazing, right? This must have blown your mind.

You have never ever have heard of these theories in reality checks. Let me tell you, our brain has not yet evolved as much as it did 100 years ago. Yeah, we invent and develop new things, but **our emotions still remain the same.**

2.7 Answering "HOW TO" Questions ⟶ Quick Guide

"Brand is just a perception, and perception will match reality over time."

– Elon Musk

How to judge Potential Brand Value:

Superior Products/Services: For instance, Jio disrupted the Indian telecom industry with its affordable plans, leading to a subscriber base of over 400 million by 2020.

Unique Selling Points: Patanjali's focus on Ayurvedic and natural products caters to a growing market segment conscious of health and wellness.

How to Create Strong Brand Relationships:

- **Articulate Brand's Nature:** Tata, known for its ethical standards and social responsibility, has consistently ranked high in consumer trust.

- **Align Internal Processes:** This ensures every aspect of the business reflects the brand's values and promises.

- **Construct Brand-Centric Experiences:** Amul's unique advertising and product range create a distinct brand experience, resonating with a broad customer base.

- **Connect Brand with Rituals:** Rituals create a sense of belonging; for example, many Indian families start their day with Amul butter or milk.

- **Community of Believers and Non-Believers:** Building a brand community involves engaging loyal customers while also addressing the concerns of skeptics.

How to do Evidence-based Marketing:

- **Market Research:** Flipkart's early adoption of Big Data analytics helped them understand and cater to diverse consumer preferences.

- **Targeted Advertising:** Using specific consumer data to create personalized advertising campaigns.

How to do Strategic Assumptions for Branding:

- **Brand Differentiation:** Differentiating your brand in a crowded market is essential, as seen in the diverse product offerings of companies like Tata and Reliance.

- **Improve Loyalty:** Loyalty programs and customer engagement strategies can significantly enhance brand loyalty.

How to do Brand Revitalization:

- **Enter New Markets:** Indian brands like Zomato and Ola are expanding globally, entering new markets and broadening their customer base.

- **Target New Segments:** Identifying and catering to emerging consumer segments can rejuvenate a brand.

- **Increase Usage Frequency:** Encouraging more frequent use of products/services can boost sales.

- **Change Product Quantity:** Adjusting product sizes or quantities can meet changing consumer needs, as seen in various FMCG products.

How to do Brand Repositioning:

- **Image Repositioning:** Redefining the brand's image to stay current with trends.

- **Market Repositioning:** Shifting focus to new market segments when needed.

- **Product Repositioning:** Adapting products to better suit consumer needs or preferences.

- **Total Repositioning:** Sometimes a complete overhaul of the brand is necessary to remain competitive.

How to do Raising Brand's Profitability:

- **Raise Prices:** Implementing strategic pricing based on value perception, not just cost.

- **Cut Costs:** Efficient cost management can significantly improve profit margins.

- **Rationalize Product Range:** Focusing on the most profitable products can streamline operations and enhance profits.

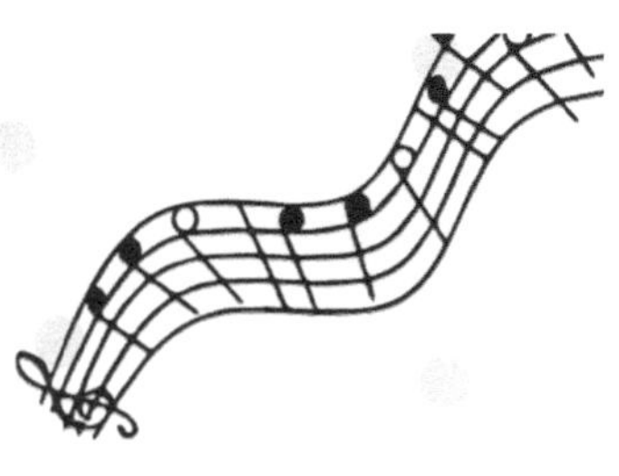

ADVERTISING

3. Advertising

3.1 Advertising: What is a Good Ad?

"The best ideas come as jokes. Make your thinking as funny as possible."

– David Ogilvy

Same Image, Every year…

Same Video, Every year…

Like people, products too have a personality. By now, you might have gotten the gist because you just covered branding and how the brain works, right?

Why does advertising mean a lot?

Why am I discussing it here now?

Because I want to complete what you, as owner, founder, dreamer, and builder, do, I want to take this time and read this chapter with the ultimate thought of grabbing the market.

In a nutshell, Advertising means to be OVER-SIMPLIFYING THE COMPLEXITY

You know, people don't have enough time to see your blaabbbb.

Now. I will give you numbers on why advertising is still a big part of lead generation for any industry. With over 65% of global ad expenditures by 2024, this is a clear indicator of the ongoing shift from traditional to digital media. This trend reflects changing consumer behaviors, where people are spending more time online, particularly on mobile devices.

According to research, there will be $205.4 billion in social media ad spending via mobile by 2027. This trend is likely driven by the high engagement and effectiveness of mobile ads.

Despite the rise of digital media, television remains a significant medium for advertising. While its growth is slower compared to digital, it still shows an increase, indicating that TV continues to be an important channel for certain types of advertising campaigns.

The drop in ad spend in 2020 due to the pandemic was significant but not as drastic as initially expected. This resilience might be attributed to businesses adapting quickly to the new environment, perhaps by shifting more towards digital advertising, which can be more targeted and cost-effective.

3.2 Unleashing Your Inner Creative Genius for Advertising Success

"In the world of Internet Customer Service, it's important to remember your competitor is only one mouse click away."

– Doug Warner

Let's dive into a fascinating journey where we unlock the hidden treasure of your mind—the subconscious. In the bustling world of advertising, it's not just about selling products; it's about weaving stories that resonate. And guess where these stories come from? Your subconscious mind!

Think of your subconscious as a powerful ally, quietly working in the background while you're busy with your daily hustle. It's like a creative powerhouse, waiting to unleash groundbreaking ideas. Remember the iconic Amul ads? They're not just witty; they're a brilliant play of subconscious creativity.

You need to feed your mind with a rich diet of information. Read, observe, and absorb everything around you. The vibrant streets of Mumbai, the colorful festivals, the daily struggles and triumphs of people—all these are fodder for your creative mind.

Now, here's the secret sauce – relaxation. Ever noticed how great ideas pop up when you're taking a leisurely walk or enjoying a cup of chai? That's your subconscious saying hello! It's crucial to unwind and give your mind space to wander.

Practical Steps to Creative Nirvana:

- **Info Feast:** Be curious. Read, watch, listen, – soak in as much as you can.

- **Chill Mode:** Find your zen. Walk, meditate, or just daydream.

- **Patience is Key:** Good ideas need time to brew, like a perfect cup of masala tea.

- **Stay Open:** Your next big idea might just be waiting at the corner chai shop!

- **Your Rituals:** Create your own rituals. Maybe it's a morning walk or jotting down thoughts in a journal.

Alright, here's something crucial – patience and persistence. Great ideas, like the majestic Taj Mahal, aren't built in a day. **Your subconscious mind is an artist, not a machine.** It needs time and space to be created. So, don't rush it.

The journey of Dhirubhai Ambani wasn't overnight; it was a saga of persistence and belief in his vision. Similarly, nurture your ideas with patience. If they don't strike gold today, they might tomorrow. Trust the process and keep at it. Your big advertising breakthrough is waiting just around the corner, ready to dazzle the world!

Remember, your subconscious is your silent partner in this exciting journey of advertising. Nurture it, and it will reward you with ideas that not only sell but also tell stories that touch hearts and minds across India.

The following questions will help you determine whether you have a brilliant idea:

- Is it creating love at first sight for me?

- Is it unique?

- Is it the perfect strategy?

- Is it worth the next 5 years?

3.3 Laws of Powerful Advertising

"Nobody counts the number of ads you run; they just remember the impression you make."

– Bill Bernbach

This chapter was named after the ultimate 48 laws of power because that book got me thinking and I realized that it was going to be advertising complete. I will make analogies and bridge the gap between the two books so that you get what you need to do for your advertising.

The misconception is that advertising is gambling, but it is all about our psychology and evolution. What have we been observing from the sage, where we used to hunt and now live in big cities in skyscrapers? So I am not going to give you anything aside from the fundamentals of having big and good ads.

"Make others come to you - Use bait if necessary."

Do you know that advertising ultimately creates jobs for salesmen? If perfected, this can work as a salesman for you. You need to study the product before you are going to advertise. The more you know about it, the more likely you are to get the BIG IDEA. As a successful salesman knows their customers, you need to find the answer, "Would it help me sell them if I met a buyer in person?"

Keep it simple. Remember, the best ideas are often the easiest to understand, like the straightforward taglines of Fevicol. People remember very little. Do not make to amuse your audience. If you want to entertain, make movies. You don't need applause; you need sales.

How do you find out about your audience?

- Go out in person and sell before you create Ad

- Conduct surveys to learn the attitude of the buyers. [Do not guess.]

"Re-Create yourself"

You need to make the product the hero of your advertising. Re-create your product by forging a new identity—one that commands attention and never bores the audience. If your competitors are making the same good product as yours, then do not try to be better. Just make ad about 'what's good about your product—do it clearly and honestly.' Adapt and evolve with your market. Look at how Reliance Jio changed the telecom landscape.

Your image is your personality. You have to decide how you are going to use your brand image. The personality of a product is a mixture of its name, packaging, price, style, and the product itself.

"Court attention at all costs."

You need to get the attention of your audience. The purpose of headlining is to pick out people you can interest. Even with commercials, I have seen people skim over the ads you run on social media platforms. Headlines on ads are headlines on news items. We, as humans, are selfish. We will not read for amusement. We will glance, and we want to be amused or benefitted.

Steps to get the perfect attention:

- Use high picture quality image.

- Different platform can have different headline but same content

- Your idea should be remarkable so that your subject becomes outstanding

- Like an iPhone, if you don't have story, make your package the subject of illustration

- Before-After images are attention appealers

- You can also grab attention with scratch board drawings

- If you have a Brand Font or character like McD has a joker, recall that in your ads

- Focus on single persona rather than crowd.

- If you have a human face in your ads, make its height real Do not enlarge it

- Faces which make people think "Awww" will grab attention like baby face, dogs, etc.

- If you use photo of men, women will ignore them. If you use photos of women, men might ignore your ads

- A colourful Ads can become memorable

- Ride the wave of current trends, but with your own unique twist.

"Give something to get something."

The essence of human nature hasn't changed much over millennia; what worked a thousand years ago often still applies today.

Reciprocity always works. "Think of it as 'give and take.' In India, for example, when you walk into a store and are offered a free sample, it's more than just a nice gesture. This strategy can lead to actual sales. It's like getting a taste of Basundi before deciding to buy the whole bowl."

"Trailer creates curiosity; movies spark value."

In the dynamic world of marketing, understanding and leveraging human curiosity is akin to harnessing a powerful force. Just as a tantalizing movie trailer captivates and intrigues an audience, your advertisements should spark that same level of interest. This innate curiosity, when effectively tapped into, can transform passive viewers into engaged potential customers. Moreover, the art of advertising lies in storytelling; a narrative that takes the consumer on a journey is far more compelling than mere facts and figures. An advertisement that tells a story, much like a well-crafted car commercial that takes the audience on an emotional or aspirational drive, resonates deeply and can significantly enhance consumer engagement.

In the Indian market, the perception of value plays a critical role. Consumers seek quality and value, preferring products that offer a luxury experience without breaking the bank. It's not just about finding a bargain; it's about feeling like they've accessed the best, akin to the thrill of getting an iPhone during a Diwali sale.

Pricing strategies can significantly influence this perception. A product like Patanjali, for instance, brilliantly balances affordability with the allure of quality, demonstrating the impact of strategic pricing. Furthermore, exclusivity in offers, such as VIP access or limited-edition products, creates a sense of special privilege and belonging among consumers. And when it comes to claims about your product, specificity is key.

A claim that is backed by clear, concrete reasons, much like Amul's explanation of why their butter is superior, holds more weight and is more persuasive to the discerning customer.

Understanding Consumer Habits

- **Changing Habits:** "Altering consumer habits is challenging and costly. It's easier to tap into existing habits than to create new ones."

- **Problem Solving vs. Prevention:** "People are more likely to act to solve a problem than prevent one. Marketing should focus on solutions, like Dettol does by emphasizing its effectiveness against germs."

- **Exclusivity in Pricing:** "Products priced above average can be positioned as luxurious or elite, much like how an Audi is perceived compared to a standard sedan."

- **Consistency in Branding:** "Never alter your brand's core message. Consistency builds trust, just like Tata has maintained its image for decades."

- **Power of Testimonials and Demonstrations:** "Testimonials, especially from loyal customers, can significantly boost credibility. Demonstrations, like live cooking shows promoting a non-stick pan, let people see the product in action."

Influencer Marketing

"Utilizing influencers effectively can massively amplify your brand's reach. Think of how celebrities endorsing a product instantly grab attention, like Shahrukh Khan in Byju's ads."

Emotional Connection in Advertising

"Connecting emotionally with your audience is vital. Remember the Vodafone ZooZoo ads? They weren't just selling a service; they were telling a story that touched hearts."

3.4 The Art of Effective Advertisement: A Guide for Indian Entrepreneurs

"What really decides consumers to buy or not to buy is the content of your advertising, not its form."

– David Ogilvy

To create an engaging and conversational adaptation of Nick Kolenda's insights on advertising psychology suitable for an Indian audience, we'll break down the key points into digestible segments with added context and examples relevant to Indian culture and market trends.

Unlock the secrets to crafting advertisements that not only catch the eye but capture the heart and mind of the Indian consumer. As an entrepreneur in India's vibrant marketplace, understanding the art of advertisement is crucial. This chapter is a tapestry of psychological insights, creative strategies, and cultural nuances, all woven together to help your ads resonate deeply with your audience.

1. Understanding People: The Core of Connection

In the diverse cultural landscape of India, your advertisement's success hinges on relatability. Choose models that reflect your target audience, creating an instant connection. For products associated with virtue, employ direct eye gazes in your ads to foster trust and authenticity. Understanding your audience is the first step in crafting a message that resonates.

2. Words & Impact: Crafting a Memorable Symphony

Words in your advertisement are more than text; they are emotional catalysts. Amplify the impact by focusing on words that carry emotional weight, making them larger to trigger a stronger response. Slogans and calls-to-action benefit from a touch of creativity – think rhyme and rhythm. A catchy, rhyming slogan isn't just heard; it's remembered.

3. Color Psychology: Painting Emotions

Color plays a pivotal role in how your ad is perceived. Use grayscale to highlight problems, creating a visual contrast that emphasizes the effectiveness of your solution. In text-heavy ads, a restrained use of color prevents overwhelming your audience, allowing your message to stand out.

4. Images & Perception: Visual Storytelling

Images are the silent narrators in your advertisement. Position them strategically on the left side of your ad to engage the right hemisphere of the brain, which is better at processing visual information. On the right, use a visual stopper to keep the viewer's gaze from drifting away, ensuring they absorb your entire ad narrative.

5. Framing Techniques: The Art of Storytelling

Leverage the power of negative framing to grab immediate attention, but quickly balance it with a positive resolution to maintain engagement. Conversely, use positive framing to ensure your message sticks in the audience's memory. The art of framing is about controlling the narrative lens through which your audience views your ad.

6. Ad Mediums & Timing: Strategic Placement

The choice of ad medium and the timing of its release are crucial. Ensure your ad's medium aligns with the state your audience is likely to be in when they encounter it. Spread your ads over time to enhance effectiveness; repeated and spaced exposure embeds your message into the audience's psyche.

Applying These Principles in the Indian Context

Imagine a scenario where an Indian startup is launching an organic skincare line. They could use these techniques, as follows:

Images & Perception: The ad can start with a left-sided image of someone enjoying their natural environment, creating a connection with nature and wellness.

Color Psychology: Challenges like pollution or skin damage could be shown in grayscale, contrasting with the colorful vibrancy of the solution—the skincare products.

Words & Impact: Using emotionally resonant words like 'pure', 'natural', or 'revitalizing' in a larger font will resonate more. A catchy, rhyming slogan can make the brand memorable.

Understanding People: Featuring everyday Indian people in the ads, with direct eye contact, can create a connection with potential customers.

Framing Techniques: The ad might start with a negative framing of the problem (e.g., skin damage due to pollution) but end on a positive note showing the benefits of the product.

Ad Mediums and Timing: Online video ads can be effective if targeted when the audience is likely to be thinking about skincare, such as in the evening or during beauty-related content browsing.

By weaving these principles with elements familiar to Indian consumers, such as cultural cues and local storytelling, businesses can create more impactful and resonant advertising campaigns.

As we conclude this chapter, remember that effective advertising in India is not just about selling a product; it's about telling a story, building a connection, and embedding your brand into the cultural narrative. In the next chapter of "Zero to Everyone," we dive into the copywriting realm. Stay tuned as we journey through the exciting world of marketing, transforming every reader into a maestro of the Indian marketplace.

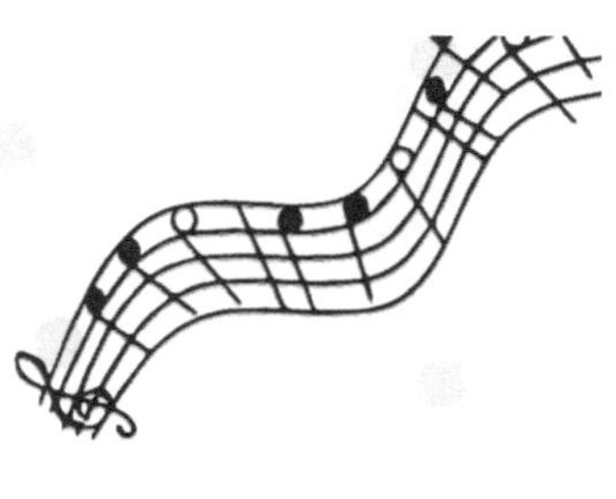

COPYWRITING

4. Copywriting Methods

In "Zero to Everyone," we embark on a journey through the vital realm of copywriting. It's an art, a science, and a crucial skill in the arsenal of any entrepreneur or marketer aiming to make an impact. This chapter isn't just about writing; it's about crafting messages that resonate, influence, and convert. Let's dive into the world where words are not mere strings of letters, but powerful tools that shape perceptions, build relationships, and drive action.

The Essence of Copywriting

At its core, copywriting is about understanding your audience's needs, desires, and pain points, and then communicating your message in a way that is not only heard but felt. It's about striking a chord with your readers, making them feel understood, and guiding them toward a solution – your product or service.

Crafting the Message

The key to effective copywriting lies in the balance between clarity and creativity. Your message should be clear and straightforward, but it should also be engaging and memorable. This balance is achieved through a deep understanding of your audience and a creative approach to language.

Emotional Connection

One of the most powerful aspects of copywriting is the ability to create an emotional connection with your audience. This involves using language that evokes emotions – whether it's happiness, relief, excitement, or even fear, as long as it's relevant and authentic. Emotional connection can transform a simple message into a compelling story, making your brand memorable and relatable.

The Art of Persuasion

Copywriting is essentially about persuasion – convincing your audience to take action, whether it's to buy a product, sign up for a service, or simply engage with your brand. This requires an understanding of psychological triggers such as authority, scarcity, urgency, and social proof. By weaving these elements into your copy, you can effectively influence decision-making.

Clarity and Conciseness

In a world bombarded with information, clarity and conciseness are paramount. Your copy should be easy to read and understand, free from jargon or complex language. Every word should serve a purpose, whether it's to inform, persuade, or entertain.

SEO and Digital Copywriting

In the digital age, copywriting extends beyond traditional mediums. It's crucial to understand the principles of SEO (Search Engine Optimization) to ensure that your online content is not only compelling but also discoverable. This means using keywords strategically, structuring your content for readability, and creating copy that resonates with both humans and search engines.

Continuous Learning and Adaptation

Copywriting is an ever-evolving field. As markets change and new trends emerge, it's important to keep learning and adapting your approach. This includes staying updated with the latest digital marketing trends, understanding new consumer behaviors, and continuously refining your writing style.

4.1 Revealing Hidden Truths about Copywriting

"Copy is a direct conversation with the consumer."

– Shirley Polykoff

Think of copywriting as the art of persuasion, but in a subtle, engaging way. The trick is to make your audience act without them realizing they're being persuaded. Consider the iconic ads by Fevicol—they're not just selling adhesive; they're telling a story that resonates with everyone. It's about crafting messages that speak directly to the audience in a language and tone that feel familiar and friendly, much like a heartwarming conversation over a cup of masala chai

The Law of Three and the Five Whys Technique

Imagine you're a detective trying to solve a mystery - that's exactly what the 'Law of Three' and the 'Five Whys' technique is like in marketing. It's about peeling back the layers to uncover the real issues customers face. In India, take the example of OYO rooms. They asked 'why' to understand the inconsistency in budget accommodations and revolutionized affordable hospitality. [Why1 $\longrightarrow$ Why2 $\longrightarrow$ Why3 $\longrightarrow$ Why4 $\longrightarrow$ Why5] It's about asking the right questions to really get to the heart of customer pain points, like a chai seller keenly observing which blend his regulars prefer.

Without a strong reason, people do not buy. We need to bond with multiple reasons why people buy *[covering here again]*:

- **Emotional Satisfaction:** People often buy products to fulfill emotional needs, such as happiness, security, comfort, or love. Purchases can be driven by the desire to feel a certain way.

- **Self-Expression and Identity:** Products can be a way for individuals to express their personalities, beliefs, and values. People may purchase items that they feel represent who they are or who they aspire to be.

- **Pleasure and Enjoyment:** The pursuit of pleasure is a strong motivator. This includes the enjoyment derived from luxury items, hobbies, entertainment, or indulgences like gourmet food.

- **Social Status and Prestige:** Many purchases are influenced by the desire to enhance one's status or prestige in the eyes of others. This includes buying luxury brands, the latest technology, or high-status items.

- **Self-Improvement and Aspiration:** Consumers are often motivated by the desire to improve themselves. This could be through educational materials, health and fitness products, or tools that enable the acquisition of new skills.

- **Psychological Reward:** The feeling of reward or accomplishment can motivate purchases, such as buying something after achieving a personal goal or as a form of self-reward.

- **Fear and Security:** Purchases are sometimes motivated by fear or the need for security. This can include buying insurance, security systems, or products that ensure health and safety.

- **Curiosity and Exploration:** A desire for new experiences and exploration can drive purchases related to travel, books, new technologies, or novel products.

- **Nostalgia and Sentimentality:** People may buy things that remind them of a cherished past or to recapture memories, leading to purchases of vintage items, antiques, or products associated with childhood.

- **Escapism and Stress Relief:** Products that offer a form of escapism or stress relief, such as video games, spa products, or travel, can be motivated by the desire to take a break from everyday life.

Addressing Fears, Speaking to Desires

Your content should be a mirror reflecting your customers' fears and desires, like talking to a friend who really gets you. Take, for instance, the way

Swiggy addresses the desire for convenience and variety in their campaigns. They tap into the Indian love for diverse cuisines, making it more than just a food delivery service. It's like how a wise shopkeeper in a local bazaar reads his customer's needs and offers just what they're looking for.

Understanding Audience Types: Hot, Warm, and Cold

Hot Audience: Think of them as loyal customers at your local chai stall who visit daily. They know you, follow you, and trust your brand. They're like your regulars who don't need to be convinced; they just need to be reminded and appreciated.

Warm Audience: These are the ones browsing through the aisles, interested but not yet committed. They're looking for a solution, much like someone in a bookstore searching for a specific genre. They know their problem and are actively seeking a solution. Your job is to show them why your solution is the best fit.

Cold Audience: This group is akin to a tourist in a new city. They are aware of a problem, like navigating an unfamiliar place, but they don't yet realize there's a solution. Educating and informing them is key, gently guiding them to realize how your product or service can address their unacknowledged needs.

Creating the Ideal Customer Avatar: Akash

Now, let's create a persona for each type. Let's call our ideal customer 'Akash.' To make Akash come alive, think deeply about what he wants, thinks, and says.

To fully understand and cater to each type of Akash, engage in live interactions, observe customer behavior, participate in forums, analyze queries on your website help desk, study your popular products, conduct surveys, and monitor social media conversations. This approach is like a shopkeeper in a local market who knows exactly what to offer each customer who walks in, based on their regular purchases, queries, or even their confused expressions.

Crafting Great Headlines

"Headlines are crucial. Use formulas like 'Who Else Wants...?', 'They Laughed When I...', 'Do You Make These Mistakes in...?', 'How to Get... Without...', 'Discover How To...', 'Would You Like To...?', 'Caution: Don't Let This...', and 'If You Can..., I'll Show You How You Can...' to grab attention. It's like how catchy Bollywood movie titles get us intrigued."

4.2 The Art of Copywriting: Crafting Words That Resonate

"People don't buy for logical reasons. They buy for emotional reasons."

– Zig Ziglar

Vividness: Painting with Words

- **Imagine the Unseen:** Just like how Amul vividly describes its butter, use simple, imaginative words. Instead of saying "enhance your cooking," say "add a golden touch to your parathas."

- **Concrete over Abstract:** Swap vague phrases with specific examples. Instead of "quality service," say "24/7 customer support with a 5-minute response time."

- **Scenario-Specific Language:** Relate to your audience's world. For a monsoon sale, say, "Waterproof your wardrobe with our rain-friendly collection."

- **Product Applications:** Like Swiggy mentioning specific food items for late-night cravings, use examples your customers can taste, smell, or feel.

- **Immersive Hypotheticals:** Engage consumers by asking, "Imagine sipping Darjeeling tea in the serene hills of Himachal?"

- **Positive Imagery:** Use affirmatives. Say, "Our packaging is 100% recyclable," not "Our packaging doesn't harm the environment."

- **Semantic Connectivity:** Link words like a chain of related ideas, enhancing the impact and recall value.

Continuity: Crafting a Seamless Narrative

- **Active Voice Dominance:** Like Tata Steel's slogan, "We also make steel," use active voice for directness and clarity.

- **Connective Tissue:** Bind your sentences with words that flow like a river – use 'and', 'because', 'therefore'.

- **Subject Continuity:** Start new sentences with the subject of the previous one for smooth transitions.

- **Unambiguous Writing:** Ensure clarity. Avoid sentences that can be interpreted in multiple ways.

Framing: Shaping Perceptions

- **Segmentation:** Address different needs separately. A page for small businesses and another for corporations, like Flipkart does for its diverse consumers.

- **Autonomy Respect:** Empower choice. Remember the successful Cadbury campaign, "Kuch Meetha Ho Jaye?" It suggested, not imposed.

- **Indirect Benefit Description:** Highlight benefits subtly. Don't just say, "This car is safe." Show it's awarded for safety standards.

- **Acknowledging the Other Side:** Be transparent. Mention both pros and cons, like many online shopping reviews.

- **Rhetorical Engagements:** Ask questions. "Ever thought of owning a home in Mumbai?" It gets people thinking.

- **Impact on Others:** Show how choices affect others. "By choosing our electric scooters, you're contributing to cleaner air in Delhi."

Linguistics: The Power of Language

- **Semantic-Linguistic Alignment:** If your service is fast, the sentence should be short and snappy.

- **Descriptive Proximity:** Keep descriptive words close to their subjects. "Silky-smooth sarees," not "Sarees that are silky smooth."

- **Alphabetical Sequences:** Use phrases with a rhythmic alphabetical flow for a pleasing effect.

- **Imperfect Verbs for Action:** Use ongoing verbs to create a sense of action. "Creating smiles with every delivery."

- **Diverse Language:** Mix it up. Combine short and long sentences with different emotional tones, like a well-composed song.

- **Phonetic Flow:** Ensure your words are as easy on the tongue as they are on the ears.

- **Exclamation Economy:** Use exclamation marks sparingly. Let your words carry the excitement.

- **Humanizing Products:** For loyal customers, humanize your products. Like how Micromax calls its phones "your perfect companion."

The essence of impactful copywriting is making every word count, painting pictures with phrases, and speaking directly to the heart of the consumer. It's about creating a connection that goes beyond the product, tapping into the emotions and imaginations of your audience. With these techniques, you can write copy that not only sells but also builds lasting relationships with your customers.

4.3 Problem-Agitate-Solution PAS-formula

"A copywriter should have an understanding of people, an insight into them, a sympathy toward them."

– George Gribbin

In this chapter, you are going to be mind blown by the art of using the PAS framework. Believe me, it is such a powerful persuasion technique that it might also cause harm. You need to carefully use it in your content copywriting.

A great deal of sales copy can be generated using this framework. Some of you might think this is just copying the framework and using it. It's killing our creativity. But what about the formula you use in mathematics? It does help to solve bigger and newer problems, right?

Similarly, using the PAS framework will not diminish your creativity; it will actually help you create better persuasive content.

As per the headline, you already know PAS stands for Problem - Agitate - Solution. So as layman terms you can think it as a:

- **Problem:** Identify the problem or challenge that your audience is facing. This helps to establish credibility and create a sense of empathy with your audience.

- **Agitation:** Agitate the problem by highlighting the negative consequences of not solving it. This helps create a sense of urgency and motivates the audience to take action.

- **Solution:** Present your solution as the answer to the problem. This helps to provide value and demonstrate the benefits of your product or service.

Now let's dig deep into each one of them, starting with the problem. It is easy to identify the problem.

Show them their problem. Now, how do you do that? It depends on how creative you can be. Let's say you identify a problem as "Fat and unhealthy body". You cannot directly address that problem because shy people who will be your customers will not come forward. Try something like "Unhealthy diet causes people obese". These people can resonate and will actually read your content further.

Your headlines should be complete and make the claim that it is related to the problem. It should actually resonate with the audience more.

It's time to dive into the problem. That means you need to agitate the issue so much that it starts to create frustration in the minds of prospects. That's correct; you need to bring in emotion here. A lot of emotion will come into play so that your copy gets a sale.

How can you make sure your content has such pieces in it?

First of all, it depends on how well you have researched the issue. The first layer of the issue is given by everyone, but what about level 7 of the same issue? Can you go to that? Let's take the above example in detail.

What if I say that "a person who is depressed more and feels lonely eats more. Because they generate stress hormones. This not only affects the body but also the mind as well. Your loved ones might feel you are not making any progress in any activity. Looking like an obese person does naturally make it in mind that person cannot run or walk. And when you go the gym everyone sees you in a very different way"

This agitates the problem, right? How were you feeling after reading that? In this sense, you have to hit all the possible pain points you can think of.

There are a few different ways that you can **agitate the problem** when writing copy:

- **Highlight the negative consequences of not solving the problem:** Show your audience how the problem is impacting them and how it will continue to do so if left unaddressed.

- **Use strong, emotive language:** Use words and phrases that create a sense of urgency and stir up emotion in your audience.

- **Use storytelling:** Tell a story that illustrates the problem and the negative consequences of not solving it. This can be a powerful way to create a connection with your audience and motivate them to take action.

- **Use statistics and data:** Share statistics and data that illustrate the scope and impact of the problem. This helps to establish credibility and create a sense of urgency.

Here comes the final part of the PAS framework. You need to provide a solution. Will you directly present your solution to the customer? Here are the benefits and features of using your services.

Nope, never do that. Instead, show them

You need to show them that your solution makes their lives easier. That is what they are looking for. Every customer or prospect is reading your copy not because of your features, but because they are looking for what it is for them. They are looking for their solution.

So bring it to them As per the example taken above, you can say like: "The app will give you regular reminders for the meals and water intake. With clean meals optimized using your data you just have to follow what the app is saying. When you do that you are already halfway to your weight loss journey."

By using these techniques, you can effectively agitate the problem and create a sense of urgency in your audience, which can motivate them to take action and seek out a solution.

"A problem well put is half solved."

– John Dewey

4.4 Is your Secret Safe?

Of course not. Do you really believe that when you tell someone your secret, it will stay with them for the rest of their lives?

Come on, man! Get real. This will never happen.

Let's suppose I tell my friend I am dating someone, and I don't want to shout it out loud as this is the initial phase. This friend of mine has a girlfriend; do you still believe my secret is going to remain there?

No right. So another day I went to college, and I got a message from some random guy wishing me luck. When I checked, it appeared to be the girl's ex. And how did he get to know? You guessed it right, my close friend

So this quality of a human being is worth leveraging. People like to share information because it makes them likable, and everyone craves that. Some people may want to share secrets in order to feel closer to someone or to gain their trust, while others may want to share secrets in order to receive emotional support or advice. Additionally, people may also choose to share secrets because they feel a sense of relief.

The most powerful marketing technique is to put words in the mouths of prospects. Yes, when your audience is talking about your product and service, it is selling itself.

Word-of-mouth marketing (WOMM) is the technique of advertising a product or service through happy consumers' personal recommendations. Because it is generally viewed as more trustworthy and real than other types of promotion, WOMM may be a very powerful marketing technique for firms.

Leverage that in your content copywriting. You can tell a story about how happy your customer was. People like stories, and it motivates others to do the same. If I told you my story, I would say that I was depressed about my weight until one day I made some decisions that caused things to change. My life started to change. Now, I live a healthy life and have six-pack abs.

Give people a way to make themselves look good while promoting their products and ideas all along the way.

You need to build a strong brand name. Apple is a well-known brand. Content should be made so that it positions you differently from others and makes you visible with your brand. Brands that provide excellent customer service are more likely to receive positive word-of-mouth recommendations.

When you have delivered everything, your content should make the prospects feel a sense of community. Every brand does it. If you take the fitness industry, people call themselves "groups of like-minded people." Tagline of cult fitness is "We are cult". Or Apple makes sales like they show in advertisements with sophisticated men walking alone and not with a crowd.

Brands that create a sense of community around their products or services are more likely to generate positive word-of-mouth recommendations.

This type of content gets more attention and generates more leads.

4.5 Adaptable Personality

"Adaptability is not imitation. It means power of resistance and assimilation."

— Mahatma Gandhi

It is amazing to know that different brands have different personas. You might have seen several cases where this was implied. You need to tailor your voice according to the brand; that's what makes you a fantastic content copywriter. This can also involve adjusting your language, tone, and word choice to better align with the target audience and the overall feel of the campaign. Yes, you need to make sure which type of audience you are referring to.

You have many impressionists who mimic the voices of different personalities, which is the same thing you need to do with your writing.

Let's take an example of the different voices of different brands:

- **Nike:** You can feel that it is bold and energetic. Mostly because it focuses on athletes and their potential. Nike catchphrase also says, "Just do it."

- **Apple:** A well manner sophisticated voice that reflects sleek design and innovation. They have pretty straightforward language that focuses on benefits and features of their products.

- **Starbucks:** How do you feel when I take their name? You always feel friendly, welcoming, and cozy, right? This is what they use to focus on a brand's voice that reflects a welcoming atmosphere. They often use phrases like "We're here to inspire and nurture the human spirit—one person, one cup, and one neighborhood at a time."

By adapting your personality to your copywriting, you can better connect with your audience and effectively communicate the message you want to convey.

Molding yourself into the character will help you become something else. This is what a good content copywriter does. In content copywriting, "brand personality" refers to the unique character and tone of the brand that are reflected in its written content. A brand's personality can be conveyed through the language, tone, and style of its copy, as well as through its visual identity and overall aesthetic.

A clear and consistent brand personality is important for building an identity, positioning you differently from competitors, and establishing an emotional connection with the audience.

Your writing should trigger the imagination of the reader. They must follow the path you showed in your content. One great way to do this is to use metaphors or analogies. By using these literary devices, you can help your readers better understand and visualize your message.

Visual media can be a powerful tool for triggering the imagination and helping readers visualize what you are writing about. Use high-quality images and videos to illustrate your points and help readers see what you are describing.

Your audience should be engaged in your content, like you are talking to them. Encouraging discussion and debate can also be a great way to get readers engaged with your content. Another way is to tell a relatable story.

Use storytelling techniques to engage your readers and help them visualize the events and characters in your story. Use descriptive language and details to create a sense of place and help readers feel like they are part of the story.

Tips for writing like you talk:

- **Use simple, familiar language:** Avoid using jargon or overly complex language, and instead opt for words and phrases that you would use when speaking to someone in person.

- **Use contractions:** Using contractions, such as "I'm" instead of "I am," can help make your writing sound more natural and conversational.

- **Use short, simple sentences:** Short, simple sentences are easier to read and can help make your writing feel more conversational.

- **Avoid formal language:** Formal language can feel stiff and distant, so try to avoid it in favor of a more casual and friendly tone.

- **Use active voice:** Using the active voice, where the subject is performing the action, can make your writing more engaging and easier to follow.

The idea is for your writing to sound like a natural conversation, so be yourself and use your own voice.

4.6 A/B Testing

"Do not… address your readers as though they were gathered together in a stadium. When people read your copy, they are alone."

– David Ogilvy

You might be wondering why there is such a delay. Well that's so you guys get what you need.

Wait there!

I think you might be tired because there has been no lead generation or customer engagement.

Well, this is a common question that we face generally, and we don't know where to begin. No issues, I am here to tell you secrets that no one shares openly. This secret test is called A/B testing.

You might be wondering, "What the hell is A/B testing?"

Everyone knows how to apply A/B testing, and you have been using it since your childhood. I am not joking. So, let me ask you a big question here? Have you not created any backups for yourself anywhere? I think not.

Let's talk about those career decisions you made. You were already thinking about choosing a path, and you were good at that. At the same time, you had a Plan B to try out in parallel to gauge your interest. This is used in marketing or content copywriting as well.

A/B testing, also known as split testing, is a method of comparing two versions of a piece of content to see which one performs better. The goal of A/B testing is to increase engagement, conversions, or other metrics of interest by making data-driven decisions about the content.

This testing is a randomized experimentation process where you have two versions with some change in a variable. It helps to understand engagement, churn, impact, etc. Both work with different sets of people, and data metrics are noted to see which one is performing better.

Do you not like to be data driven?

Research shows that 70% of the initiatives fail because they are not taking advantage of data. We all want to use technology, but that is of no use if you are not making sure of that. There is a high chance you are going to miss out. So what do I learn from this?

Learning is not yet complete.

A/B testing will eliminate all the guesswork, which saves a lot more in investment. Now, this can be either time, money, or effort. Here A refers to the control or the original testing variable, and B refers to the testing or a new version of the original testing. By comparing the performances of the two groups, it's possible to determine which version of the content is more effective.

The control group: This group represents the original version of the content and serves as a benchmark for the performance of the other group. The control group is used to establish a baseline for the metrics being measured, such as engagement or conversions.

The treatment group: This group represents the modified version of the content and serves as a test to see if the changes made have a positive impact on the metrics being measured. The treatment group is the version of the content that is being tested against the control group.

During the testing period, the two groups are exposed to their respective versions of the content, and the metrics are tracked and analyzed. The results of the test are then compared between the control group and the treatment group to determine which version of the content performed better.

The variation that results in an improvement in your business metrics is referred to as the "winner." Applying the changes from this winning version to your tested content or elements can help improve your website and boost your return on investment. You can use it to get qualified leads or more sales.

How is it going to help me with content copywriting?

Yeah, this question was next for mine too. When we try some marketing campaigns, we try to make them more resonant with customers. So by testing it out, we can identify that. When it comes to content copywriting, A/B testing can be used to test things like the language used in a call-to-action button, the length of a landing page, or the tone of an email.

By testing different variations of the same content, you can identify the version that resonates most with your audience and improve the overall performance of your marketing campaigns.

It's important to note that A/B testing should be done carefully, as there can be unintended side effects, like confusing users. Also, A/B testing should be repeated multiple times with different audiences and variations of the test to see the best result. Yes, A/B testing can be applied to content writing. In fact, A/B testing can be used to test various aspects of content writing, such as headlines, subheadings, text length, tone, and formatting.

Here are a few examples of how A/B testing can be used to improve content writing:

- **Headlines:** A/B testing can be used to test different headlines to see which one grabs the most attention and encourages readers to click through to the rest of the content.

- **Subheadings:** A/B testing can be used to test different subheading styles, such as short and punchy or longer and more descriptive, to see which one makes the content easier to read and understand.

- **Text length:** A/B testing can be used to test different text lengths to see which one performs better in terms of engagement and conversions.

- **Tone:** A/B testing can be used to test different tones of writing, such as formal or informal, to see which one resonates more with the audience.

- **Formatting:** A/B testing can be used to test different formatting, such as text size, font type, color, and bold/italic.

It's important to use A/B testing in a strategic manner and test only one thing at a time. This allows you to have a clear understanding of what caused the difference in performance and make a more educated decision on how to improve your content.

It's also worth noting that A/B testing should be used in conjunction with other methods of understanding the audience, such as analytics and user feedback, as it's only one of the many factors that should be considered when creating content.

4.7 Power Words

"It is easier to tone down a wild idea than to think up a new one."

– Alex Osborn

Are you excited to learn the next secret?

I think you are.

This magic ingredient will make your content very powerful. Yes, we are talking about power words. Power words are those that help your content get attention. These words are so impactful that they create emotions in the minds of readers. Power words are used for the effective messaging you are trying to convey.

Power words are words that have a strong emotional impact and are often used to grab the reader's attention, persuade them, or convey a particular message more effectively. They can help to add emphasis, create a sense of urgency or importance, and make your writing more memorable and engaging.

For example, using powerful words like "secret," "limited," or "exclusive" can create a sense of exclusivity and make the reader feel like they are getting special access to something. Similarly, using words like "free," "save," or "new" can create a sense of value and encourage the reader to take action.

When you are aware of the audience, you can use some words that can grab their attention quickly. The key is to choose words that resonate with your audience and align with the message you are trying to convey. It's also important to use power words appropriately and not overuse them, as they can lose their impact if they are used too frequently or in the wrong context.

Your content should be able to trigger the audience's emotions. So it's more like when your friends tease you after a breakup with a girlfriend. They only use one word, and your emotions get triggered. That is, the effect should be created when using the power words.

Here are some tips for using power words in content writing:

- Small quantities. Overusing power words can dilute their effectiveness and make the writing seem forced or inauthentic.

- Right power words for the right audience. Different power words will have different effects on different readers, so it's important to choose words that will resonate with the audience and fit the tone and style of the content.

- Beginning of sentences or headlines to grab the reader's attention. This is a powerful way to draw the reader in and make them more likely to continue reading.

- To create a sense of urgency or scarcity. Words like "limited," "exclusive," and "urgent" can encourage readers to take action or make a decision more quickly.

- To describe benefits or results. Words like "incredible," "miraculous," and "amazing" can help to emphasize the positive outcomes that the reader can expect from using a product or service.

- To create a sense of emotion or connection. Words like "love," "hope," and "joy" can help to create a sense of emotional resonance with the reader.

4.8 Understandable to 5-year-old

"Tell the truth, but make the truth fascinating."

– David Ogilvy

iPhone 14 launched with an A15 bionic chip, which is manufactured at 5 nm and has an integration of 15.8 billion transistors. The 5nm system on a chip (SoC) makes it different from other processors on the market. With 6-core CPU cores, that is, 2 performance and 4 efficiency cores, making it power efficient. This bionic chip works on a 16 core neural network, which can carry out 15.8 trillion calculations per second. With 5 GPU cores, it handles the graphics very efficiently.

Now this makes the reader go out of bounds. The target audience will not find this catchy.

How about this?

Apple just launched the new iPhone 14. The processing is ultra fast for people and not droids. Ceramic Shield front, Glass back and aluminum design stand out for sophisticated people. It has graphics that make the gaming experience real. Comes in Midnight, Purple, Starlight, Blue

This content will stand out from others. It is quite straightforward for people, and the features listed. It does not give tech related information. This is just an example; people apply emotions more than referring to any technological advancement.

What have you learned from this?

You might be wondering why we have to change such a thing. Well, of course, that needs to be done because, while you might be good at technical stuff, a larger audience is not. According to a survey, 24% of people don't even know about technology or stuff. When your writing excludes such big claims and narrows it down to simple terms, it makes it more balanced and easier to understand.

How many times have you checked into such a depth of technicalities to buy something? I think never. Most of the things we buy either look good or just fit what we want. So if some content is making it too hard to explain products' advantages, it might lead to a disadvantage in sales or generate leads.

Conveying the message is not easy because the receiver has its own perception. What you want to deliver might be intercepted correctly. It is generally recommended to write in clear, simple language that is easy for the average reader to understand. This is especially important when writing for a wide audience or about a topic that may be complex or technical.

Using language that is too advanced or difficult to understand can make it difficult for readers to follow along and may discourage them from continuing to read.

Oversimplifying too much might also lead to giving the wrong message. Writing in the language of a 5-year-old does not necessarily mean using childish language or simplifying the content too much. Rather, it means using clear and concise language and avoiding unnecessary jargon or technical terms that may not be familiar to all readers.

Breaking up complex ideas into smaller, smaller chunks and using concrete examples to help illustrate points. By using this approach, you can help ensure that your content is accessible and easy to understand for a wide range of readers.

Steps you can follow to make your life easier:

- **Read your writing out loud:** It will not only help you listen to your content more clearly, but it will also make it better.

- **Use clear and simple language:** Avoid using jargon or technical terms that may not be familiar to a 5-year-old. Instead, use simple, straightforward language that is easy to understand.

- **Break up complex ideas:** Divide complex ideas into smaller, more manageable chunks. Use concrete examples to help illustrate points and make the content more relatable to a young audience.

- **Use familiar words:** Choose words that are commonly used by 5-year-olds or that they are likely to understand. Avoid using words that may be too advanced or unfamiliar.

- **Use short sentences:** Keep sentences short and to the point. This will help to make the content more manageable for a young reader.

- **Use pictures and illustrations:** Visual aids can be a helpful way to explain complex ideas or concepts to a young audience. Consider using pictures or illustrations to help illustrate your points.

4.9 What's in It for Me? (WIIFM)

"If you can't turn yourself into your customer, you probably shouldn't be in the ad writing business at all."

– Leo Burnett

When you are trying to deliver something so compelling that it gains visibility, it is still not able to convert to sales. Why? Because you are missing the most important of all, "WIIFM." It stands for "What's in it for me?". Yes, you can make something more attractive, but it misses the interest of the customer, it misses sales. Your content should deliver the solutions customers are looking for, not what you are providing.

Whether you are experienced or a beginner, you still need to put yourself in the customer's shoes. This is where you can identify whether you are able to find WIIFM. Every business wants customers to come back and have a long term business. To show them that you are the one, you need to recognize their interests. When a customer sees that content, they recognize themselves.

Different content will have a different target audience. As areas of interest differ largely with every product and service you provide, your prospects want their lives to be easier and their jobs to be done. Are you making that commitment in your copy?

Before starting your research, try looking into what your product can do for them. Yes, it will help you generate the first few leads, and eventually, after more research, you can keep updating with the pain and interest of new prospects. Your leads don't even care what you are delivering. It is the selfish intent of every human being to look out for themselves before others.

For example, how will you write content for a wireless mouse?

Tired of being tangled in wires? Resolving them requires huge patience and time. You obviously have more important work than just trying to open the knots of a wired mouse. Free movement of the mouse without any wire will make your life much easier. Take care of the important stuff, and let us take care of this.

Customers want to have personal satisfaction. Now your content can make them feel that this is what they were looking for. Your job as a brilliant writer is complete. Making customers resonate with products. You need to find out what motivates the customer.

The secret of any talented content writer is that their content already answers the questions. Your content should reveal the instances where the customer is stuck. To do that, you need to dig deep into prospects' minds. It is simply empathizing with their pain. Here, empathy has a very important role.

You also need to use words and phrases that are likely to appeal to the reader and that emphasize the benefits of your content. For example, you might use words like "free," "save," "easy," or "simple" to make your content more appealing.

To write content with WIIFM in mind, you should focus on highlighting the benefits and advantages that the reader will receive from reading or using your content. This means that you should clearly and prominently feature the personal advantages that the reader will gain from your content, and you should use language that emphasizes how the reader will benefit. Here are a few tips to keep in mind when writing content with WIIFM:

- **Identify the key benefits:** Before you start writing, make a list of the benefits that your content will offer the reader. This could include information, solutions to problems, entertainment, or any other value that your content will provide.

- **Put the benefits front and center:** Make sure that the benefits of your content are clearly stated and easy to find. This could mean highlighting them in headings or subheadings, or using bullet points to list them out.

- **Use persuasive language:** Use words and phrases that are likely to appeal to the reader and that emphasize the benefits of your content. For example, you might use words like "free," "save," "easy," or "simple" to make your content more appealing.

- **Make it personal:** Use language that speaks directly to the reader and addresses their specific needs and interests. This can help to make the content feel more relevant and valuable to the reader.

- **Test and optimize:** As with any aspect of writing, it's important to test and refine your content to see what works best. This might mean A/B testing different headlines or trying out different approaches to highlighting the benefits of your content.

CASE STUDY

5. Player BECOMES a Product: The AIR JORDAN Case Study

"Simplicity is the ultimate sophistication."

– Leonardo da Vinci

Do you know why BRANDs matter:

1. Being a PRESENCE in the minds of consumers, they exist independent of PRODUCT.

2. Their PERCEIVED VALUE in consumers mind.

3. Brands are TOOLS to help consumers make decisions.

If I just START with your all time STAR "MICHAEL JORDAN" directly I would not be doing all justice.

We all know how much of an IMPACT he has had on the lives of people and how he has become an IDOL for Basketball lovers…

Keeping that in mind, I will try to include his influence in NIKE's marketing.

In 1984, Nike had a 15% market share and was struggling to crack the basketball market.

You are aware of Nike and Michael Jordan's 1984 partnership. This RELATIONSHIP forever altered the landscape of the sports world.

It actually became a symbol of performance, fashion, and cultural influence.

We are going to convert the MAIN aspects of BRAND BUILDING that is, the brand ladder:

1. Awareness

2. Function

3. Affect-related

4. Long Term Bonding

Starting with the very first step on the ladder, "AWARENESS"

It means that the product should be present in front of the consumer. They should have the answer to the specific question, "What Is It?"

This will act as an identifier for the product. Imagine if you are living in the 1980s and have never heard of Nike and only hear on a day-to-day basis that Michael Jordan is scoring for CHICAGO BULLS. You do want to get to know him more, right?

The Air Jordan brand, launched in 1984, owes its popularity to a combination of factors.

The endorsement of Michael Jordan, an iconic NBA player, and Nike's marketing efforts played a crucial role in brand recognition.

In 1985, Nike spent $1 million on advertising for the first Air Jordan model, leading to an estimated revenue of over $100 million in the FIRST YEAR ALONE.

Stepping to the second step, which is "FUNCTION"

Oh wait, what???

Do I really need to go to that one? Where do I have to make this product explain "WHAT IT DOES?".

I don't think so…

For the sake of understanding, I will explain it to YOU. In this section, it covers the promise that BRAND is making. That means JORDAN itself means that time has become THE PRIME.

The Air Jordan's functional aspects focus on performance, innovation, and style. Nike does introduce new technologies in cushioning, support, and traction, such as the visible Air unit in the Air Jordan III (1988). Additionally, the collaboration with Tinker Hatfield, a renowned designer, resulted in iconic designs like the Air Jordan III, which featured the elephant print and the Jumpman logo.

By 2021, over 35 different Air Jordan models had been released, each offering unique performance features and designs.

Uniquely, Nike's offer included a five-year deal worth $2.5 million plus a percentage of sales from the Air Jordan line. This unprecedented contract proved lucrative, as Air Jordan became a hugely popular sneaker line.

The third STEP refers to "EMOTIONAL BENEFITS"

When you BUY something from the market, it always comes down to how emotionally attached you are to the product. If JORDAN itself became the PRODUCT, how it will be seen?

In this case, it helps to answer the specific question, "HOW IT MAKES YOU FEEL?"

Air Jordans have had a significant emotional impact on consumers.

The sneakers became a symbol of success, style, and self-expression. Owning a pair of Air Jordans made customers feel connected to Michael Jordan and his on-court successes.

A 1991 study found that 77% of young males aged 12 to 20 identified with Jordan and felt that owning Air Jordans increased their social status.

Finally, we reached the TOP, which means the brand has made the LONG-TERM BOND.

If we look deeper into this, we all want to have high STANDARD in our circle of influence.

AND how this brand is making me do so…

The Air Jordan brand has successfully fostered long-term bonding with its customers. Limited releases and collaborations with famous artists and designers (e.g. Virgil Abloh and Travis Scott) have created a sense of exclusivity and desirability, leading to a strong resale market.

According to StockX, a sneaker marketplace, the average resale price for Air Jordans in 2020 was $285, with some models reaching up to $2,000.

See to THE LEGEND…

Jordan notably wore the original Air Jordans during his last game at Madison Square Garden in 1998. In a pre-game interview, he mentioned his desire to honor the past and reminisce about the old times by donning his 1985 "Chicago" Air Jordan 1s.

However, the first generation of Air Jordans did not offer the same degree of comfort and support as their newer versions:

"It's been quite a while since I last wore them, and it's interesting to return to the court and recall the old days and the games I played here, with the shoes being a part of those memories. But, my feet are in pain."

By creating awareness through an iconic partnership, delivering functional promises, evoking emotional responses, and fostering long-term relationships, Nike and Michael Jordan have built a brand that transcends the sneaker industry and stands as a cultural phenomenon.

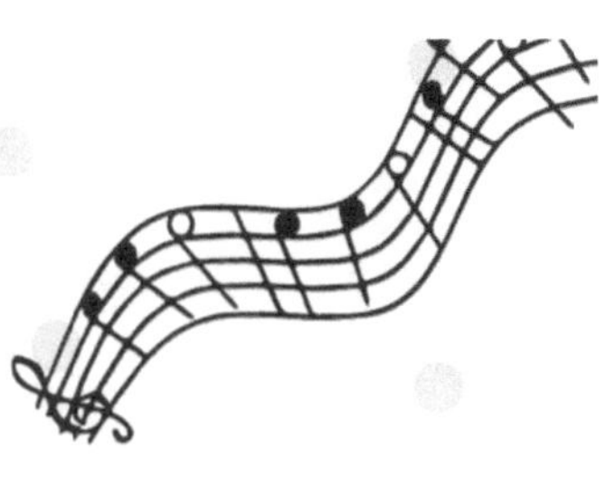

PLANNING

6. Go-To-Market Plan

"Build something 100 people love, not something 1 million people kind of like."

– Brian Chesky

Let me start with an example of what competition really means. I know many of us know the DHABA on the outskirts of the city, where mostly we go out to eat. Right? For people who don't know about Dhaba, these are like restaurants, but the vibe is totally different. As these are having the table in the open air. And the evening is like mind-blowing with typical local songs playing in the background.

These dhaba are quite cheap and give a large variety of food to drivers and also to students and bachelors because they generally prefer to go out and eat.

Can you think who is the direct competitor of this DHABA?

One level of thinking would be a Dhaba next to it or maybe a restaurant. Right?

But what if, I tell you, the competitor of this Dhaba is "Instant Noodles"? MIND BLOWN?

Why?

If people are consuming these, then no one will come OUTSIDE to eat in this dhaba. And do you market the size of instant noodles?

The global instant noodles market was valued at around $42.2 billion in 2019 and was expected to grow at a CAGR (Compound Annual Growth Rate) of approximately 5.2% from 2020 to 2027, according to a report by Grand View Research.

That is how you think OUT OF THE BOX.

What IF…

This question generally comes up when you are planning your product launch. But most startups, when starting with marketing their product, do not lay their foundation.

Like, why should their customers buy from them and not from their competitors?

I do not like you, or WHO ARE YOU?

This is the general question that will arise when your target is unaware of you.

Now, let's start with something your company should always have and should thrive for, and that is VISION. If you are clear with your vision, then only you are going to pitch and have confidence in your product.

BUT wait… I think I missed something.

Generally, startups may find it challenging to adapt to market changes, customer needs, or technological advancements. And that is why they fail immediately, just after 1-2 years of bankruptcy.

Do you know that 29% of the time you will be changing your strategies? And this is not the number I am making; this is the research from GARTNER. This is going to be a major roadblock to having the BIG SUCCESS.

Strategic planning is the cornerstone of sustainable business growth, especially for startups. This guide aims to provide an exhaustive resource on strategic planning models that can help startups scale exponentially.

Strategic planning is the process of defining an organization's direction and making decisions on allocating its resources to pursue this direction.

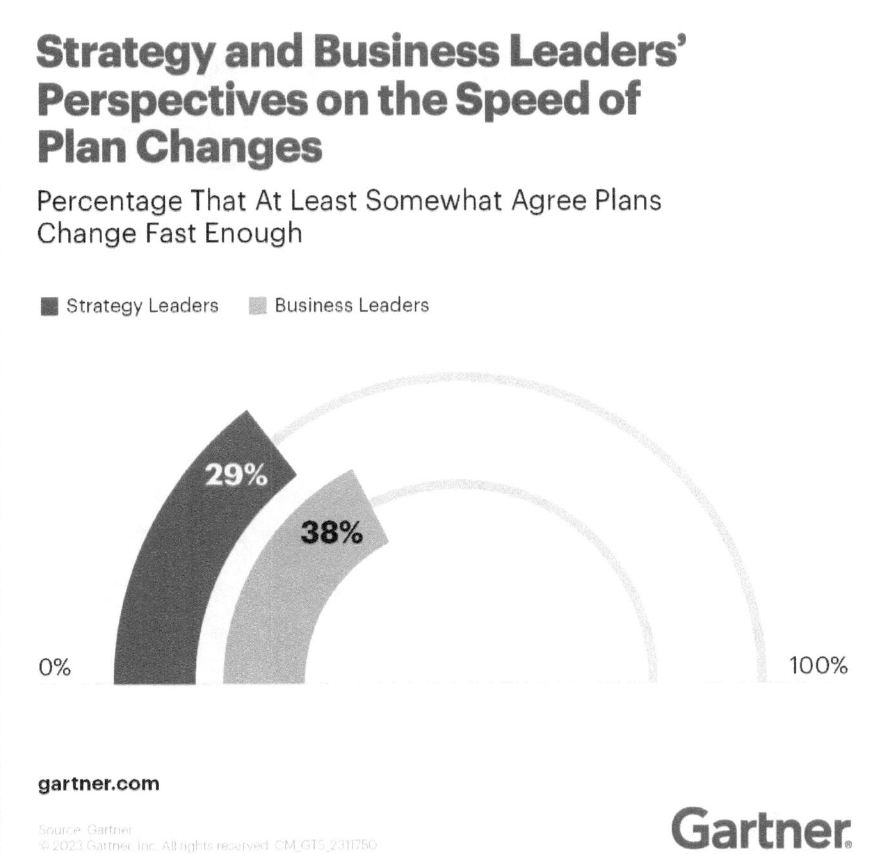

"The key is to abide by some key principles of any strategic planning process—whether at the enterprise, business-unit or functional levels," says Marc Kelly, VP at Gartner. "And eliminate everything that isn't necessary and sufficient to communicate an effective strategy."

I will give you certain components which you need to set up for your MARKETING your product.

Step 1) Define your EXPECTATION

Step 2) Vision Statement *(what you want to be in future)*

Step 3) Mission Statement *(It focuses on the present and serves as a guide for decision-making)*

Step 4) Goal *(Individual or combined undertakings that, when achieved, drive differentiated value in the longer term.)*

Step 5) Objective *(measurable goals that a company aims to achieve in a specific timeframe.)*

Step 6) Assess your capabilities *(generate a prioritized list of functional capabilities to bolster or gaps to fill as a result of your findings.)*

Step 7) Develop a tactical plan *(They are short-term plans that focus on specific departments or teams within the company.)*

Step 8) Develop an action plan *(Action plans are the most detailed level of planning, specifying the exact activities that need to be completed to achieve the tactical plans and, by extension, the strategic objectives.)*

Step 9) Set measures and metrics *(Measures allow you to evaluate the efficacy of your action plans. A metric describes the actual data collected to quantify the measure)*

These 9 steps may seem overwhelming but believe me this is going to deal maker for your STARTUP. Do not get confused, just flow instructions blindly and you will definitely achieve the SUCCESS.

Startups are more vulnerable to market fluctuations, competition, and other external factors. If you are not strategizing the marketing plan way before you want to go to market you will fall through the cracks, leading to delays and inefficiencies.

BUT, if I am here do not be afraid.

Strategic planning helps startups:

- Align resources
- Mitigate risks

- Capitalize on opportunities

- Create a competitive advantage

Now it's time to give you the MODELS, which BIG COMPANIES use till today.

SWOT Analysis: SWOT stands for Strengths, Weaknesses, Opportunities, and Threats. It's a framework for identifying and analyzing these four aspects of your business. Conduct a SWOT analysis at least once a year and after any significant business changes.

Case Study: Apple

Apple's strengths in design and weaknesses in pricing, opportunities in wearables, and threats from competitors like Samsung.

PESTLE Analysis: PESTLE stands for Political, Economic, Social, Technological, Legal, and Environmental factors affecting your business. Use PESTLE to scan the external macro-environment in which your startup operates.

Case Study: Uber

Uber's challenges with legal regulations and its opportunities in technological advancements like autonomous vehicles.

Balanced Scorecard: This model focuses on four perspectives: Financial, Customer, Internal Processes, and Learning and growth. Implement key performance indicators (KPIs) for each perspective of the balanced scorecard.

Case Study: Starbucks

Starbucks uses a balanced scorecard to measure customer satisfaction, financial performance, and employee training.

Blue Ocean Strategy: This strategy involves creating a new, uncontested market space rather than competing in saturated markets. Identify the factors that make your market competitive and think about how you can redefine them

Case Study: Bewakoof

Bewakoofl created a new market space by redefining the T-shirt experience, focusing on adults rather than children.

These are some of the models you can use to plan your strategies. You may need to use a combination of these models to create a comprehensive strategic plan.

DO NOT GET SCARED!!!

Most of the time, you just and it also depends on your research before start planning. And you will know which will suit your PRODUCT. Make sure you have a timeline to deliver with responsibilities assigned. Keep on tracking the progress. With your Key Performance Indicators (KPIs), Return on Investment (ROI) and Customer Satisfaction Surveys

How to Choose the Right Model?

Factors to consider:

- Industry

- Stage of Business

- Business Goals

- Available Resources

Strategic planning is not a one-time event but an ongoing process. Upcoming chapters aims to be a comprehensive resource for startups looking to implement effective strategic planning models for exponential growth.

Mission Statement Development Exercise

Step 1: Core Values Identification

- List your business's core values:

    - ____

    - ____

    - ____

Step 2: Business Goals

- Outline your primary business goals:

    - ____

    - ____

    - ____

Step 3: Audience Understanding

- Describe your target audience:

    - Who are they? ________________________

    - What do they value? ________________________

    - ____

Step 4: Unique Selling Proposition (USP) Analysis

- What makes your business unique?

    - ____

Step 5: Drafting the Mission Statement

- Combine insights from above to draft your mission statement:

    - ____

    - ____

Step 6: Review and Refinement

- Reflect on the draft. Does it align with your values and goals?

    - Yes/No (Circle one)

    - Notes for refinement:

    - ____

Step 7: Feedback Gathering

- Share your draft and note down feedback:

    - Feedback Summary:

    - ____

Step 8: Finalization and Implementation

- Final Mission Statement:

    - ____

    - ____

Implementation Plan:

- How will you incorporate this mission statement into your business operations?

    - ____

Note: Keep this exercise as a dynamic tool. Revisit and revise your mission statement as your business evolves.

6.1 Niche: The Riches are in the Niches.

"People spend money when and where they feel good."

– Walt Disney

Till now, your head might be exploded with so many things. Believe me, we have much more interesting topics to cover.

I have understood the importance of fitness at the age of 24, I think. I was way heavy—around 95 kg. But it was hard work I had to do to get in shape. But believe me, this chapter is not about how I got fit 😃. It is something much deeper.

As a fitness enthusiast myself, I was on the hunt for the perfect whey protein supplement. My journey to find the right product led me to an eye-opening realization about the intricacies of marketing strategies and how products are positioned to appeal to core human desires: health, wealth, and relationships.

One sunny afternoon, I found myself browsing through the aisles of a local health store in Bangalore, surrounded by an array of whey protein products.

Each brand claimed to be the best, boasting benefits like muscle gain, quick recovery, and improved strength. But as I scrutinized the labels and marketing slogans, **I began to see a pattern.**

It dawned on me that these products weren't just selling whey protein; they were strategically positioned to tap into the core desire of health, specifically targeting fitness enthusiasts like me.

But there was more to it. Each brand had carved out its niche, addressing specific submarkets within the health domain.

For instance, one brand positioned itself as the go-to choice for serious bodybuilders, emphasizing high protein content and muscle-building properties. Another focused on the busy professional, promoting its product as a quick, convenient source of nutrition. Yet another brand targeted the weight loss market, highlighting how their formula could help shed fat while preserving muscle.

This segmentation was a classic example of the "Product $\longrightarrow$ Core market $\longrightarrow$ Submarket $\longrightarrow$ Niche" strategy in action. The core market was health supplements, the submarket was whey protein, and the niches varied from bodybuilding to weight management.

As I stood there, a tub of whey protein in hand, I realized how my own preferences were being influenced by these marketing tactics.

I wasn't just looking for a health supplement; I was searching for a product that aligned with my personal fitness goals and lifestyle.

This revelation changed my perspective on marketing and consumer behavior. I understood that successful products don't just meet a general need; **they speak to specific desires and carve out a unique space in the consumer's mind.**

In the end, I chose a whey protein supplement that resonated with my personal fitness journey – one that promised not just muscle growth but also aligned with my holistic approach to health and wellness.

This experience was a lesson in the **power of targeted marketing and the importance of understanding the deeper desires that drive consumer choices.**

Now let's pin down methods to find your NICHE

Before moving forward, keep in mind that you are becoming focused on a specific customer with a specific need. Before you ask these questions, you have to back out of our main niche and back to the submarket. You need to pull people from the submarket into your new niche, so these questions relate to the people in the submarket.

As we delve into the realm of marketing, especially in the vibrant and diverse Indian market, it's essential to understand the significance of focusing on a specific customer with a unique need.

Let's have a conversational journey through this process, exploring key questions that can help refine your marketing strategy. Imagine we're sitting in a cozy café in Bangalore, sipping chai, and discussing these pivotal questions:

Question #1: What specific problem does your product or service aim to solve?

Question #2: Do the individuals in your target market show an irrational level of passion or interest?

Question #3: Are your potential customers both willing and financially able to spend on your offerings?

Question #4: Would your niche opportunity generate excitement among people in the broader submarket?

Question #5: In what ways does your product or service enhance the lives of your customers?

Question #6: Can you share proven results or successes that your product or service has achieved?

Question #7: Where have you observed the best results or highest impact of your product or service?

Question #8: What common issue is your product known for solving effectively?

Question #9: What distinct features and benefits does your product have over competitors?

Question #10: If customers were to purchase your product for just one key benefit, what would that be?

Here's something to always keep in mind: the market is like a river, constantly flowing and changing. It's essential to regularly circle back to those key questions about your niche. Why? Because as your business grows and evolves, so does the market. You'll likely introduce new products or features, and you need to stay sharp and innovative to keep pace.

Imagine you're juggling more than one niche. That's when it gets really interesting. You'll need to figure out which of your products fits in each niche. It's like having different conversations with different groups of friends. You tailor your stories (or in this case, your marketing messages) to resonate with each group. That's how you make the most of each niche, ensuring your message hits the right note every time.

Niche Identification Worksheet

- Core Market

  - Health

  - Wealth

  - Relationships

- Submarket (Select or Define)

  - Example: Health ⟶ Weight Loss

- Niche (Specific Focus within Submarket)

  - Example: Weight Loss for College Students

- Target Audience Characteristics

  - Age Range: _______

  - Interests: _______

  - Challenges: _______

  - Location: _______

- Market Demand Analysis

  - Online Search Trends

  - Social Media Discussions

  - Competitor Analysis

- Unique Value Proposition

  - What makes your offering unique in this niche?

  - Unique Aspect: _________

- Product/Service Ideas for Niche

  - Idea 1: _________

  - Idea 2: _________

  - Idea 3: _________

- Customer Pain Points & Solutions
  - Pain Point 1: _________ $\longrightarrow$ Solution: _________
  - Pain Point 2: _________ $\longrightarrow$ Solution: _________
- Potential Barriers to Entry
  - Barrier 1: _________
  - Barrier 2: _________
- Initial Marketing Strategies
  - Strategy 1: _________
  - Strategy 2: _________

6.2 Target Audience Identification and Segmentation [Whom to Sell]

"Good marketing makes the company look smart. Great marketing makes the customer feel smart."

– Joe Chernov

The market consists of many types of consumers, products, and needs. You must determine which segment offers the best opportunities. Every market has segments, but not all ways of segmenting are useful. It should be like consumers responding in a similar way to marketing efforts as it happens in the case of medicines.

Imagine you're setting up a business. Your first big decision?

Figuring out what you're going to sell and to whom. This is where market segmentation becomes your best friend.

Think of 'market segmentation' as 'market sorting.' It's like sorting a big, diverse crowd into smaller, more manageable groups.

Imagine market sorting as dividing a large crowd into smaller groups based on what they like or need. Why do this? It's simple: it helps you customize your products or services to fit the specific tastes and needs of different groups. For instance, a clothing brand might focus on trendy, urban styles for young professionals in cities while offering more traditional, comfortable attire in rural areas.

Market sorting isn't just about getting to know your customers better; it's also about smart business. Different groups of customers think differently about prices. By sorting your market, you can set the perfect price for each group, boosting your profits.

Here's something interesting – even if your business is small, you can still be a leader in a smaller group. By focusing on a specific group, you can stand out in that area, even if you're not the biggest player in the overall market.

And there's more—market sorting can help you keep customers for the long haul. As people's lives change, so do their needs. If your products or services change with your customers' life stages, they're more likely to stay loyal to your brand.

So, when you're setting up your business, especially in a vibrant and varied market like India, your first major decision is about what you're selling and to whom.

In this exciting chapter, we're going to dive into some really crucial aspects of shaping your business. The one big question that will help you in segmentation is, "Is your target audience large enough to support your business goals?"

We'll also explore common segmentation tactics and strategies. This is all about dividing your market into approachable chunks, making your marketing efforts more focused and effective.

So, are you ready to embark on this journey with me?

If you're diving into the world of business marketing in India, understanding consumer segmentation is crucial. It's like knowing your guests before throwing a party—you need to know what they like, how they behave, and what makes them tick. So, let's break it down.

- **Profile Variables:** Think of these as basic information about your consumers. It's like knowing someone's name and hometown, but not really what they love to do. In India, this could mean knowing your consumer is a young professional from Mumbai. It's helpful, but it doesn't tell you much about their shopping habits. [There is a range of demographic, socio-economic and geographic segmentation variables in this category.]

- **Behavioral Variables:** Now we're talking actions! This is about understanding how consumers behave—what they buy, how often they shop, and why they choose one product over another. For instance, consider how often a family in Bangalore orders groceries online versus visiting a local market.

- **Psychographic Variables:** Here, we dive deep into their psyche. What are their attitudes, opinions, and interests? It's like understanding why a retiree in Kerala prefers reading a newspaper over browsing news on a smartphone. This information helps you figure out their lifestyle and buying patterns.

Think of segmentation as a creative art. You can mix and match these variables to get a clearer picture of different market segments. Let's say you're in the air travel business in India. You could segment your market by why people travel (business vs. leisure) or what they're looking for (budget travel vs. luxury experience).

Remember, there's no fixed rule on which variable to start with. You might first look at what benefits your consumers want (like fitness enthusiasts in Delhi looking for a gym). Then, add more layers like age, gender, or location to fine-tune your understanding.

By combining these variables in innovative ways, you can uncover new market segments, even in traditional markets like the saree industry in Varanasi. It's all about understanding your consumers in a way that lets you tailor your products and marketing strategies to meet their specific needs.

Diving into the world of business marketing in India? It's essential to understand who you're selling to.

Let's explore the different ways to segment your customers under profile variables:

- **Demographic Segmentation: This includes age, gender, and family life cycle.**

  Age: People's needs evolve with age. For example, what a 20-year-old college student in Pune might look for in a product is different from what a 40-year-old parent in Surat might need.

  Gender: Men and women often have distinct preferences. A young woman in Bangalore might be drawn to different marketing messages than a middle-aged man in Jaipur.

  Life Cycle: Each stage of life brings new needs and spending habits. A newlywed couple in Hyderabad might spend differently than retired individuals in Kochi.

- **Socio-Economic Segmentation: This is about classifying people based on their occupation, education, and income.**

  In India, this might mean categorizing a software engineer from Gurugram differently from a teacher in Bhopal. Their income levels, example, their educational backgrounds, and hence, their spending habits and priorities, can vary widely. For example, you can make a table like this below to organise your audience.

Social Grade	Social Status	Occupations	Examples	Approx. Percentage of Households
A	Upper Middle Class	Higher Managerial/ Professional	Doctors, Lawyers, Professors, Corporate Executives	3%
B	Middle Class	Intermediate Managerial	Managers, Teachers, Software Engineers	10%
C1	Lower Middle Class	Junior Managerial, Supervisory, Clerical	Junior Executives, Bank Clerks, Salespersons	24%

Social Grade	Social Status	Occupations	Examples	Approx. Percentage of Households
C2	Skilled Working Class	Skilled Manual Labour	Electricians, Mechanics, Artisans	30%
D	Working Class	Semi-Skilled and Unskilled Manual Labour	Factory Workers, Construction Laborers	25%
E	Subsistence	None	Pensioners, Casual Workers, Unemployed, Students	8%

- **Geographic Segmentation: Where people live can hugely influence their preferences and needs.**

For instance, consumer preferences in urban areas like Mumbai or Delhi can be vastly different from those in rural areas or smaller towns like Varanasi or Ludhiana.

- **Geodemographics: This combines geographic data with demographic and socio-economic information.**

In India, this could mean understanding that neighborhoods in South Mumbai have different consumer profiles compared to those in East Delhi, influencing everything from retail store locations to targeted marketing strategies.

Segment Type	Description	Indian Examples	Statistics/References
Demographic	Age, Gender, Life Cycle	College student in Pune, Parent in Surat, Retiree in Kochi	India's median age is around 28 years, indicating a young population. Gender ratio is approximately 1.08 males/females (Source: Census of India).

Segment Type	Description	Indian Examples	Statistics/References
Socio-Economic	Occupation, Education, Income	Software engineer in Gurugram, Teacher in Bhopal	India has a growing middle class, estimated to be around 40% of the population. IT sector employees account for a significant portion of the urban middle class (Source: NASSCOM reports).
Geographic	Location	Urban areas like Mumbai vs. smaller towns like Varanasi	Urban population constitutes about 34% of the total population, with a growing trend towards urbanization (Source: World Bank).
Geodemographics	Location + Demographics + Socio-Economic	South Mumbai neighborhoods vs. East Delhi neighborhoods	South Mumbai is known for higher income levels and a higher concentration of white-collar professionals compared to East Delhi, which has a more diverse socio-economic profile (Source: Indian real estate market reports).

- **Behavioral Variables in Business Marketing**

This is all about why people buy what they buy and how they use it.

Benefit Segmentation: This is about understanding the 'why' behind a purchase. For example, in India, people might buy a smartphone for different reasons: a student in Delhi might want a phone with a good camera for social media, while a businessman in Mumbai might prioritize a long battery life for work. By understanding these benefits, companies can tailor their products more effectively.

Usage Segmentation: Here, we categorize customers based on how often they use a product or service. Think of it like tea consumption in India. Some people are heavy tea drinkers, needing several cups a day, while others might only have it occasionally. Identifying these patterns helps businesses focus on their most frequent users.

Purchase Occasion: Some purchases are tied to specific occasions. In India, buying gold jewelry is popular during weddings and festivals like Diwali. Stores can capitalize on these occasions by offering special deals or introducing new designs.

- **Psychographic Variables in Business Marketing**

  Moving on to psychographic variables, it's like painting a detailed picture of a customer's lifestyle, attitudes, and personality.

  Lifestyle Characteristics: In India, a young professional living in a metro city like Bangalore might have a very different lifestyle compared to someone living in a rural area. Their activities, interests, and the media they consume will vary greatly.

  Attitudes and Personality: Attitudes towards products and services can vary greatly. For instance, a fitness enthusiast in Pune might prioritize health and fitness products, while a tech-savvy individual in Hyderabad might be more inclined towards the latest gadgets.

Activities	Interests	Opinions	Demographics
Work	Family	Themselves	Age
Hobbies	Home	Social Issues	Education
Social Events	Job	Politics	Income
Vacation	Community	Business	Occupation
Entertainment	Recreation	Economics	Family Size
Club Membership	Fashion	Education	Dwelling
Community	Food	Products	Geography
Shopping	Media	Future	City Size
Sports	Achievements	Culture	Stage in Life Cycle

Understanding the Table:

Activities: This column represents what people do in their daily lives, such as work, hobbies, and entertainment. For example, someone's leisure activities like sports or club memberships can indicate their lifestyle and preferences.

Interests: This reflects what people are interested in or care about, ranging from family and home to fashion and food. Understanding a person's interests can help tailor marketing messages that resonate with their preferences.

Opinions: The beliefs or viewpoints people hold on various topics such as politics, social issues, or economics. This can be pivotal in understanding consumer values and attitudes.

Demographics: This includes basic statistical data about individuals, such as age, education, income, and family size. Demographics can offer a foundational understanding of a consumer's potential needs and lifestyle.

Remember, the key in psychographic segmentation is to understand not just who your audience is, but what they care about and how they live their lives. This approach enables more personalized and effective marketing strategies.

After all this work you should name your segments as individual identity, which means give them some name. Creating personas is crucial in marketing as they represent detailed customer profiles, and help you to understand specific needs and preferences. It will enable you to get targeted and personalized communication, ensuring messages resonate with the intended audience.

By reflecting real customer segments, personas will guide your product development and enhance customer experiences. They focus marketing efforts on profitable segments, optimizing resource allocation. Personas also foster empathy among business teams, ensuring customer-centric decision-making.

Target Audience Identification Exercise

Product/Service Description

Describe Your Product/Service: _______________________

Segmentation Table *[Fill out the following table to understand your target audience better]*:

Segmentation Category	Options/Characteristics	Your Selection (%)
Age Range	Silent (1928-1945), Baby Boomer (1946-1964), Gen X (1965-1981), Millennials (1982-1996), Gen Z (1997-2010), Gen Alpha (2011+)	
Geographic Location	[Specify Locations]	
Gender	Male, Female	
Type	End User/Consumer, Other Businesses	
Frequency	Year Round, Seasonal, Monthly, One Time	
Average Income (₹)	Under 25,000, 25,000-50,000, 50,000-75,000, 75,000-100,000, 100,000-150,000, 150,000-200,000, 200,000+	
Educational Level	High School, College Graduate, Post Graduate	
Social Media Sites	Facebook, Pinterest, Twitter, Instagram, Snapchat, YouTube, TikTok	
Professions	[List Professions]	
Purchasing Habits	Describe typical purchasing behaviors	
Buying Power	Describe the buying capability	
Pain Points You Are Solving	Describe the problems your product/service solves	
Secondary Target Markets	Describe any secondary markets	

Customer Persona Creation

Based on the selected segments, create a customer persona. Give them a name and describe their characteristics, needs, and preferences.

Persona Name: _______________

- Age Range: _______________
- Geographic Location: _______________
- Gender: _______________
- Type: _______________
- Frequency of Use: _______________
- Income Level: _______________
- Education Level: _______________
- Preferred Social Media: _______________
- Profession: _______________
- Why they need your product/service: _______________

Target Audience Strategy

Selected Target Audience: _______________

- Reason for Selection: _______________
- Proposed Marketing Strategies: _______________

6.3 What is so Unique about YOU?

"The aim of marketing is to know and understand the customer so well the product or service fits him and sells itself."

– Peter Drucker

Think of this as setting up your stall in a crowded bazaar.

How do you get people to stop at your stall and not just walk by? This is what positioning in marketing is all about.

Picture this: you're at a market, and there are two stalls selling cars - one is a Volvo, known for its safety and durability, and the other is a BMW, famous for its performance. These brands have carved a niche in people's minds, just like how Amul has become synonymous with dairy products in India or how Tata is recognized for its reliability.

Now, there are different ways to make your stall, or brand, stand out. It could be through the product itself, like how Heinz ketchup is known for having no artificial stuff. Or, it could be about the benefits, like how Volvo emphasizes safety. Think of how Bisleri has positioned itself as a safe and pure drinking water choice.

You can also stand out based on when or how your product is used. For instance, the convenience of 24/7 stores like Apna Bazaar in India. Or who uses it—like how Himalaya targets those who prefer herbal products.

Then there's the image you create. Harley Davidson, for instance, is all about that free-spirited, tough vibe. Or where it's from—like how German cars are seen as a symbol of engineering excellence.

And of course, there's competition with others. Pepsi, for instance, positions itself as the young, cool alternative to its rivals.

Now, to make your product stand out, it's crucial to be **credible, competitive, consistent, and clear**. It's hard to believe a nuclear power plant is eco-friendly, right? Or how Herbal Essences shampoo stood out in the US with its natural ingredients.

Some say to focus on one unique thing about your product. But sometimes, it's more than just one thing. Like Volvo, known for both safety and durability.

Wait, there's another side to this – distinctiveness. This isn't about being different in function, but in appearance or association. In India, think of how different fast-food chains like McDonald's and KFC have their own unique styles yet offer similar kinds of food. It's not always about being unique; sometimes, it's about being visible and familiar.

So, when you're setting up your marketing strategy, remember that it's not always about being different. Often, it's about being visible and memorable. Like the golden arches of McDonald's or the iconic blue of Tata.

And remember, this doesn't apply to everything. For some big, important purchases or specialized services, being unique does matter. But for most products, think about fitting in while also standing out in your own way.

Competitive advantage

Alright, let's dive into a concept crucial for your business journey - competitive advantage. Imagine you're playing a game of cricket. Having a competitive advantage is like having the best batsman or the fastest bowler on your team. It's that special something that puts your company ahead in the game of business.

There are four main types of competitive advantages you should know about:

- **Economies of Scale:** This is like buying in bulk. The more you produce, the cheaper it becomes per unit. Think of how big textile companies in India benefit from mass production.

- **Customer Captivity:** This is when your customers stick with you, not just because they love your product, but because switching to another brand is either too costly or too much of a hassle. Like how many people stick to their mobile networks or banking services.

- **Enforced Competitive Advantage:** This is like having a unique recipe or a secret technique. It's something that only you can offer, and others can't easily copy or match.

- **Technology Advantage:** Imagine having the latest tech in your arsenal. This could be cutting-edge software for IT companies or advanced machinery for manufacturing units.

Now, why should you convert this advantage into a monetary value?

Well, it's like knowing the worth of your star player in terms of runs or wickets in a cricket match. It helps you understand how much your advantage really contributes to your business.

Let's take an example. Consider Coca-Cola's brand value. It's not just about the taste; it's also about the calories and the enjoyment people get from it. Now, if Pepsi offers the same but at a cheaper rate, you need to figure out how much money you're saving or losing in this scenario.

Remember, if money isn't a part of your value proposition, focus on what makes your product or service compelling for your audience. It's about finding and showcasing that unique factor that makes your customers choose you over others.

6.4 Simplicity of Your Message: What to say to Customer

"Creativity without strategy is called 'art.' Creativity with strategy is called 'advertising.'"

– Jef I. Richards

Understanding the 'Why' Behind Your Product

Imagine you're at a bustling market in Mumbai, surrounded by countless vendors. What makes you choose one over the other? It's often their compelling story about why their product is the best choice. That's exactly what your business message should do.

Your message should be clear: it should explain not just what your product is, but why your customers, let's say the busy software engineers in Bengaluru or the thriving small business owners in Jaipur, should choose it. This is the core of effective communication in marketing.

Crafting a Great Message

1. **Speak Their Language**: Use terms and phrases that resonate with your target audience. Think of how Flipkart tailors its messaging to be relatable to the everyday Indian shopper.

2. **Highlight the Problem and Solution**: Like how Zomato identifies the hassle of cooking and offers a convenient solution with food delivery.

3. **Communicate Value Clearly**: What are you offering? How does it ease your customer's life, like Paytm simplifying online payments?

4. **Direct and Simple Call-to-Action**: Make it easy for your customers to understand how they can purchase your product.

Work on Messaging: A Structured Approach

- **Identify Key Features:** Look at what features your audience cares about. For instance, if you're selling a smartphone, is it the camera quality that your customers in Delhi talk about, or the battery life that people in rural areas value?

- **Link Features to Advantages:** For each feature, identify its advantage. A long battery life means less frequent charging, crucial for power outages common in many parts of India.

- **Analyze the 'So What':** For each advantage, ask 'So what?'. This leads you to the benefit. Longer battery life means staying connected with family or being available for business calls.

- **Create a Feature-Advantage-Benefit Table:** This helps in visualizing how each feature translates into real benefits for your customers.

Grouping Benefits and Mapping Values

- **Theme-Based Grouping:** Organize the benefits by themes. For instance, if you're selling eco-friendly products, themes could be sustainability, cost-effectiveness, and health benefits.

- **Persona Mapping:** Align these themes with different customer personas. A young entrepreneur in a city like Pune might value cost-effectiveness, while a family in Kerala might prioritize health benefits.

- **Conversion Tracking:** From Lead to Customer

So What? ⟶ Analysis

You know these characters from "The Big Bang Theory": Sheldon and Leonard. If you don't know them, go and watch Big Bang Theory and stop watching Pogo. That was a joke! Don't take that seriously. Sheldon was super in physics and zero in emotional knowledge, whereas Leonard was good in physics, not as much as Sheldon, but he was very good in emotional intelligence.

When you try to sell a product, let's say PlayStation, to both of them, how would you approach it?

Think over it; I will wait.

Have you completed your thinking? I hope so. When I am going to sell anything to Sheldon, I will try to give level -1 benefits to PlayStation. As an example, I would say that when you play with the latest PS5, you won't be facing lags, saving you time and frustration, so you can use that time for your research. This might be intimidating because Sheldon is more of a tech person, but remember that he is also a human with a little less emotional connection. But everyone does look for benefits on some level.

Now, look at how to make a sale to Leonard. This might be a little tricky because he is emotional, and you need to trigger that. That means you have to go deeper into the benefits. I would say to him, "Play with your special friend, and she might love you for this awesome time together." And definitely, Leonard is going to buy it. Ah! You must be wondering why Leonard would buy it. Go and watch The Big Bang Theory, and you'll know why.

Got any idea of what I am trying to tell you?

If not, don't worry. Don't put much pressure on I am here to tell you. **People don't buy features; they buy benefits**. What it means is that when you try to sell by showing off the feature, you might end up losing prospects. But if you go one level into the benefits of that feature, Bam! you've got yourself a deal. To do that, you have to use this amazing hack, "So What?"

When you ask "So what?" to your feature, you will get answers that you never thought of. Believe me, try it, and you will get the best answer. That can be your sales pitch, your sales copy, or anything else. You need to sell the result, not the product. If I say that features are important, you will agree with me, but never use them as a hook.

It is a common mistake for businesses to assume that their products do not have personal benefits. By focusing solely on the technical features of a product, they may miss out on the emotional and personal benefits it can provide to customers. This can make it difficult for them to effectively market the product and connect with potential buyers.

For example, a business that sells a new technology for home security systems may focus on the technical aspects of the product, such as its advanced sensors and remote control capabilities. However, they might miss the emotional benefit of giving their customers peace of mind and security in their own homes. By highlighting these benefits in their marketing, they can better connect with potential customers and increase the chances of making a sale.

It's important for businesses to understand that every product has personal benefits, it's just a matter of identifying and emphasizing them in their marketing and communication strategies.

Features don't sell but benefits do

This statement is generally true, as people are often more interested in the benefits a product can provide than its specific features. When making a purchase, consumers want to know how a product will improve their lives or solve a problem they are experiencing.

By highlighting the benefits of a product, a company can effectively communicate to potential customers how the product will meet their needs and improve their overall experience.

Let's create a "So What" analysis table for an iPhone. This table will demonstrate how a feature of the iPhone translates into an advantage and how this advantage can be interpreted into benefits for the user. We'll go through three levels of "So What" to deeply understand the impact of each feature.

iPhone "So What" Analysis Table

Feature	Advantage	So What ⟶ Benefit 1	So What ⟶ Benefit 2	So What ⟶ Benefit 3
High-Quality Camera	Captures clear, detailed photos	So What? Enables professional-level photography.	So What? Memories are captured in stunning detail.	So What? Enhances social media posts and engagement.
Long Battery Life	Lasts longer on a single charge	So What? Reduces the need for frequent charging.	So What? Reliable for long trips or busy workdays.	So What? Saves time and increases convenience.
Retina Display	Crisp and vivid visual output	So What? Improves the viewing experience for media.	So What? Reduces eye strain during prolonged use.	So What? Enhances user engagement with the device.
Advanced Security	Keeps data safe and secure	So What? Provides peace of mind about personal information.	So What? Encourages use for sensitive tasks like banking.	So What? Builds trust in the brand and product.
User-Friendly Interface	Easy to navigate and use	So What? Makes the phone accessible to a wider audience.	So What? Reduces learning curve for new users.	So What? Enhances overall customer satisfaction.

6.5 Competition Analysis Table

Competitor	Years in Business	Location/ Places Where They Sell	Strengths (What Customers Like)	Weaknesses (What Customers Dislike)	Unique Aspects of Their Offering	Promotional Strategies	Unique Capabilities (What They Do That You Can't)	Top Selling Products	Target Market (Differences from Yours)	Price Range	Existing Sellers (Who Else is Selling Similar Products)
Competitor A	[Years]	[Locations]	[Strengths]	[Weaknesses]	[Unique Offerings]	[Promotional Methods]	[Unique Capabilities]	[Top Sellers]	[Target Market Differences]	[Price Range]	[List of Sellers]
Competitor B	[Years]	[Locations]	[Strengths]	[Weaknesses]	[Unique Offerings]	[Promotional Methods]	[Unique Capabilities]	[Top Sellers]	[Target Market Differences]	[Price Range]	[List of Sellers]
Competitor C	[Years]	[Locations]	[Strengths]	[Weaknesses]	[Unique Offerings]	[Promotional Methods]	[Unique Capabilities]	[Top Sellers]	[Target Market Differences]	[Price Range]	[List of Sellers]

6.6 Traditional or Digital

"In our factory, we make lipstick. In our advertising, we sell hope."

– Peter Nivio Zarlenga

One of my friends was looking to get married. You know that in BHARAT our relatives started to say, "Umar ho gyi hai" [It's your age to get married]. So after procrastinating on this for a long time, he started to search for THE ONE.

The Indian marriage industry is BIG, estimated to be worth around $50 billion as of 2021. From lavish weddings to intricate matchmaking, the industry is a significant part of the country's cultural and economic fabric.

If you look back in the '90s, finding the right partner was a task fraught with challenges. The process was often outsourced to well-meaning relatives, community matchmakers, or even local priests.

Families would sift through biodata—resumes for marriage—trying to find a suitable match based on caste, religion, and astrological signs.

He was still doing the same, creating a BIO DATA and processing using the TRADITIONAL approach.

As you go with that approach, it might take some time to get someone. Fast forward after 3 months of regular approach, he added to get DIGITAL. He got himself registered on all the platforms, like Shaadi.com, Jeevansathi, and BharatMatrimony. Because it has made it easier than ever to find a partner.

Moreover, he got someone who was his classmate in 5th standard. They both found each other after being lost. That connection has to happen either traditional way or digital way.

The only, thing that happened fast was because he used the DIGITAL platform more and also used TRADITIONAL in some percentages.

NOW HE IS HAPPILY MARRIED…

What have you LEARNED?

Get MARRIED 😄

Understanding the difference between traditional and digital marketing is crucial for startups looking to make a significant impact. I will try to make this more exhaustive so that you can leverage it.

What is Traditional Marketing?

Traditional marketing refers to any type of marketing that is NOT ONLINE. This includes print advertisements, billboards, flyers, radio, and television ads. Startups targeting a local audience or an older demographic may find traditional marketing particularly effective.

Examples

Billboards on highways

TV commercials during popular shows

Radio spots during peak listening times

Case Study: Coca-Cola's Billboard Campaign

Coca-Cola has been effectively using billboards to create brand awareness. Their simple yet impactful designs are a testament to the power of traditional marketing.

What is Digital Marketing?

Digital marketing encompasses all marketing efforts that use the internet or an electronic device. This includes SEO, content marketing, social media, PPC, and email marketing. Digital marketing is essential for startups looking to reach a broader, global audience and gather actionable data on customer behaviour.

Examples

Google Ads for specific keywords

Facebook Ads targeting a particular age group

Email newsletters with product updates

Case Study: Airbnb's Digital Strategy

Airbnb leveraged digital marketing by using user-generated content and social media to build trust and community around their brand.

Advantages and Disadvantages

Traditional Marketing	Digital Marketing
Advantages	Advantages
High local reach	Cost-effective
Easier for older demographics to understand	Global reach
Tangible (e.g., print media)	Easy to measure and adjust
Disadvantages	Disadvantages
Often more costly	Can be time-consuming
Difficult to measure ROI	Requires technical expertise
Limited engagement	Data privacy concerns

Now I will give you **REAL LIFE knowledge** you can use to create decisions for your strategy. You will be able to weigh the pros and cons based on your startup's specific needs, budget, and target audience.

I am giving you an example hypothetical from Coca-Cola that utilizes both digital and traditional marketing channels. How you can manage your BUDGET and make decisions. For now, try to get the gist and make something for your product as well.

Channel/Item	Investment ($)	ROI (%)	Profits ($)	Loss ($)	Leads Generated	Funnel Stages	Cost per Lead ($)	People Involved
Digital Marketing								
SEO	10,000	20	12,000	0	500	Awareness	20	SEO Team
PPC (Google Ads)	15,000	25	18,750	0	300	Consideration	50	Ad Team
Social Media	8,000	15	9,200	0	200	Engagement	40	Social Media Team
Email Marketing	5,000	30	6,500	0	100	Conversion	50	Email Team
Traditional Marketing								
Billboards	20,000	10	22,000	0	50	Awareness	400	Marketing Team
TV Commercials	50,000	5	52,500	0	20	Consideration	2,500	Ad Agency
Radio Ads	10,000	8	10,800	0	30	Engagement	333	Radio Team
Print Ads	12,000	7	12,840	0	10	Conversion	1,200	Design Team
Total	130,000		144,590	0	1,210			

SWOT Analysis for Coca-Cola's Marketing Mix

Strengths

Digital: average 20 % ROI [Easy to measure, global audience]

Traditional: average 7-8% ROI [High local reach, effective for older demographics, tangible impact.]

Weaknesses

Digital: Requires technical expertise, risk of data privacy issues.

Traditional: High cost, difficult to measure ROI, limited engagement.

Opportunities

Digital: Expanding into emerging markets, leveraging data analytics for better targeting.

Traditional: Collaborations with local businesses, seasonal campaigns.

Threats

Digital: Ad fraud, changes in search engine algorithms, data breaches.

Traditional: Rising costs of ad spaces, declining effectiveness as audiences go digital.

Combining Traditional and Digital Marketing

A multi-channel approach can often yield the best results, leveraging the strengths of both traditional and digital marketing. Consider using digital marketing strategies to complement and amplify your traditional marketing efforts.

Example

Using QR codes in print ads to direct people to a landing page.

Case Study: PepsiCo's Integrated Campaign

PepsiCo successfully integrated traditional and digital marketing in their "Pepsi Refresh" campaign, using TV spots to direct viewers to an online voting platform.

6.7 Crafting Addictive Products in the Indian Market

"The secret of all effective advertising is not the creation of new and tricky words and pictures, but one of putting familiar words and pictures into new relationships."

– Leo Burnett

Welcome, Indian entrepreneurs and marketers! Today, we're exploring the Hook Model, a revolutionary approach to creating products that people can't resist. This model is a game-changer in customer engagement and product design, introduced by Nir Eyal in "Hooked."

1. Understanding the Four Phases of the Hook Model

- **Trigger:** This is the starting point. It's about catching your customer's attention. In the bustling streets of Mumbai or the tech hubs of Bangalore, this could be as simple as a catchy billboard for Myntra during the festive season, or a timely notification from a food delivery app like Zomato when it's lunchtime.

- **Action:** Here, you make it easy for the customer to act on the trigger. For instance, the simplicity of Amazon's one-click ordering system, which has revolutionized online shopping in India, makes purchasing almost effortless.

- **Variable Reward:** This stage is about creating excitement and unpredictability. Think of how Flipkart's mystery boxes during the Big Billion Days sale keep shoppers intrigued. These rewards can be anything from discounts to exclusive access to new products.

- **Investment:** The final stage is getting the customer to invest time or data in your service. For example, LinkedIn's skill assessments allow professionals to showcase their expertise, enhancing their profiles and engagement with the platform.

2. Real-World Applications in India

- **Triggers Tailored to Indian Consumers:** Whether it's festive sales or cricket season specials, Indian companies are adept at creating triggers that resonate culturally. For instance, during IPL, cricket-related ads and promotions become omnipresent, triggering interest in related products and services.

- **Ease of Action:** Take Google Pay's seamless interface as an example. Its user-friendly design and quick payment process have made it a go-to app for digital transactions in India, from roadside vendors to upscale restaurants.

- **Variable Rewards in Indian Context:** Oyo Rooms uses this effectively by offering surprise upgrades or discounts, creating a sense of anticipation with each booking.

- **Investment for Sustained Engagement:** Apps like Cure.fit encourage users to track their fitness routines, offering personalized workout recommendations based on their input, thus building a habit loop.

3. Ethical Considerations and Cultural Sensitivity

It's imperative to use the Hook Model responsibly. While it's powerful, ethical considerations must be at the forefront, especially in a diverse and culturally rich country like India. The aim should be to enhance user experience and offer value, not exploit vulnerabilities.

4. Indian Market Success Stories

Instagram and WhatsApp in India: These apps have become ingrained in the daily lives of millions of Indians. They've effectively used the Hook Model by integrating culturally relevant features like WhatsApp's UPI payment system or Instagram's Reels which became popular after the ban of TikTok in India.

5. Statistical Insights and Current Trends

As per recent data, India has seen a significant uptick in digital engagement post-2020. For instance, there has been a [insert latest statistic] increase in online shopping and digital payments, highlighting the impact of well-implemented Hook Models.

6. The Future of Hook Model in India

Looking forward, we can expect more personalized and AI-driven triggers, especially in sectors like e-commerce and ed-tech. With India's digital landscape evolving rapidly, businesses that effectively leverage the Hook Model will have a significant competitive edge.

In conclusion, understanding and applying the Hook Model can be a game-changer for businesses in India. It's about creating products and services that not only meet the needs but become an integral part of the consumer's life. For anyone looking to make a mark in India's dynamic market, mastering this model could very well pave the way to success. Happy innovating!

6.8 Marketing MIX

*"Marketing's job is never done. It's about perpetual motion.
We must continue to innovate every day."*

– Beth Comstock

"Let's dive into the fascinating world of marketing strategy, focusing on a pivotal aspect - the marketing mix. This concept isn't just a buzzword; it's the crux of modern marketing. Imagine it as a toolbox, filled with tactical tools, that a company uses to charm its target market and deliver real value.

Now, picture the marketing mix as a quartet of variables - famously known as the 'Four Ps.' Here's a breakdown:

Product: This isn't just something you sell; it's an experience you offer. Take the Ford Escape, for instance. It's not just about nuts, bolts, and spark plugs. It's about the models, features, services, and even the warranty. It's the whole package that matters.

Price: What's the tag? That's crucial. Ford, for example, suggests retail prices for the Escape. But the actual magic happens at dealerships, where prices are negotiated, keeping in mind the economic climate and the customer's perceived value of the car.

Place: This is all about how your product reaches the customer. Ford leverages a network of independent dealerships to sell and service their cars. It's about being where your customers are and making it easy for them.

Promotion: This is where you tell your story and persuade. Ford, for instance, invests a whopping $2.5 billion annually on U.S. advertising alone. But it's not just ads; it's about engagement through social media, salespeople, and promotions that make Ford stand out.

An effective marketing strategy weaves these elements into a cohesive plan, aiming to achieve the company's goals by engaging customers and delivering value. But remember, the 'Four Ps' is just a framework, a starting point. It's not just about products; it's about experiences and services. Packaging, often questioned, is part of the product experience.

Yet, there's a twist in the tale. Some argue that the 'Four Ps' reflect a seller-centric view. In today's customer-focused world, perhaps we should talk about the 'Four As': Acceptability, Affordability, Accessibility, and Awareness. These mirror the traditional 'Four Ps' but from the customer's perspective. It's about exceeding expectations, being affordable, easily available, and making sure the customer knows and remembers your product.

So, as we explore the 'Four Ps' and 'Four As,' we realize that marketing is not just about selling a product; it's about creating a relationship with the customer, understanding their needs, and fulfilling them. It's a dance between what we offer and what the customer seeks."

Imagine you're setting up a chai stall in Mumbai. Your product isn't just the tea; it's the experience - the blend of spices, the aroma, the earthen cups. Like Amul, which isn't just about dairy products but also about quality and trust.

Then comes price. It's not just a number; it's the value your customers perceive. Think of Tata Motors, offering cars like Nano, balancing affordability and quality, catering to a wide audience.

Place is all about accessibility. It's like Flipkart, which revolutionized how products reach people's doorsteps across India, from big cities to remote villages.

Lastly, promotion. It's not just advertising; it's about connecting with your audience. Take the example of Fevicol, whose ads are not just informative but also culturally resonant and memorable.

The 4 As: A Customer-Centric Approach

In the heart of Delhi, there's a small boutique that understands its customers' needs perfectly. This is where the concept of the 4 As comes in:

Acceptability: It's like that boutique, offering products that resonate with local tastes and exceed expectations.

Affordability: Just like Jio, which revolutionized internet access by making it affordable for millions.

Accessibility: Think of local kirana stores, accessible at every nook and corner, catering to daily needs.

Awareness: It's about making your brand a household name, like how Patanjali has done through its grassroots approach.

Integrating the 4 Ps and 4 As for Successful Marketing

Creating a successful marketing mix is like making the perfect biryani. You need the right ingredients (4 Ps), cooked with the preferences of your guests in mind (4 As).

In summary, the art of marketing in India lies in blending the 4 Ps with the 4 As, creating a strategy that resonates with the Indian consumer's heart and mind. It's about building relationships, not just selling products. And that, my friends, is the secret recipe for a successful business marketing strategy in India.

6.9 Budgeting: What should I charge?

"Marketing is no longer about the stuff you make, but about the stories you tell."

– Seth Godin

After going through such planning, it always comes down to how much I charge for my product. I am using the best techniques in the world for marketing and manufacturing, depending on whether your product is physical or if you are a service provider. Pricing can be the most challenging task for your go-to-market planning. Today, the world is very dynamic, and companies face a very fast-changing pricing environment.

Price is the major factor affecting the buyer's selection. It has to be enough so that you meet your costs and your profits or expectations. For simple products, where you sell one product, it is easy to charge. But as products get more complex, like software as a service, it might be required to bundle in a way that makes more sense for customers to buy.

Your price will always fall between one that is too low to generate profit and one that is too high to generate demand. What you see does not matter, but what your customer perceives of the product will set the price. If they perceive that the price is higher than its value, it is not worth buying.

Imagine you're at a local market in India, browsing through the vegetable stalls. You spot a bunch of fresh spinach, tagged at ₹30.

Now, you're wondering, "Is ₹30 a fair price for this spinach?" Let's break it down, just like you would in your mind:

Past Experience: Think back to your last visit. How much did you pay for spinach then? Was it more or less?

Advertised Deals: Maybe you saw a flyer or a sign at another stall offering spinach at a different price. How does that compare to this ₹30?

Expectation Setting: Before you even saw the price tag, you probably had a figure in mind, right? Maybe you were thinking, "Spinach should be around ₹25 or so."

Neighbouring Competition: Look around. The stall across the aisle might have spinach too. What's their price? Is it higher or lower than ₹30?

Nearby Prices: It's not just about spinach. Maybe there are other veggies priced around ₹30. Does this make the spinach seem like a better or worse deal?

All these thoughts swirl in your head, forming a "mental benchmark" against which you're judging that ₹30 price tag. It's like a mental tug-of-war, deciding if ₹30 is a steal, just right, or a bit over the top.

Many of you might be convinced that you need to set a price when designing a good product and then determine the cost. After that, your effort will be to persuade customers to buy your product. These types of tactics can generate revenue if you know your target is searching for budget-friendly products like Indigo Airlines *[You might need to brainstorm to reduce the input costs to increase your revenue.]*

When your customer buys something from you, they exchange what we call value. So your marketing must be justified by the product's value. And hence, your pricing will be Customer-value based. The consumer will use the perceived value of a product's price, so the company will work to measure it.

[Check Fixed Costs] ⟶ [Assess Customer needs] ⟶ [Check Competition] ⟶ [Set target price to match perceived value] ⟶ [Determine costs that can be incurred] ⟶ [Design Product to deliver desired value at target price]

Now you can either make a product that is equivalent to the good value, which means from a premium product to some mid-range with quality. Or you can add more features and services to differentiate your offers and change higher processes.

Before moving forward, let's analyze the pricing or steps you can follow to create your own Excel. Assuming you have a physical product, then the line of distribution goes down to retailers. For SaaS products, it becomes quite different because direct sales or affiliates can happen on the Web itself.

Let's take an example, for the Phone company: MM Phone. To determine the final pricing they should trace as below:

Retailers ⟶ Wholesalers ⟶ Price ⟶ Breakeven Price ⟶ Value needed ⟶ Profit Addition

Fixed Costs [Do not change with production]: ₹2,00,00,000

Variable Costs [Change directly with production]: ₹1500 per unit

Total Cost = Fixed + Variable

Assuming Retailer will take a 30% margin and Wholesaler will have 20% margin. The phone company research shows that below the Maximum retail price of 50K customer is willing to purchase the product.

MRP	= ₹50,000
[Minus Retail margin of 30%]	= - ₹15000
Retailer's Cost / Wholesaler's price	= ₹35000
[Minus Wholesaler's margin of 20%]	= - ₹7000
Wholesaler's cost / Phone price	= ₹28000

We have analyzed to determine the unit volume and sales needed to be profitable give a particular price and cost structure. Which is called Break-Even analysis.

Break-Even Volume = [Fixed Costs] / [Cost of 1 unit]

= ₹2,00,00,000 / [Phone Price - Variable cost]

= ₹2,00,00,000 / [28000 - 1500] = 755 units Yearly

Thus, as give cost and pricing structure, MM phones has to sell 755 units to have a breakeven

Break-Even Sales = Breakeven volume * price = 755 * 28000 = ₹2,11,40,000

Now if your goal for profit is ₹1,00,00,000, we need to calculate the number of sales needed.

Unit Volume = [Fixed Costs + Profit] / [Cost of 1 unit] = 3,00,00,000 / 26500

= 1132 units

Total Sales = 1132 * 28000 = ₹3,16,96,000

By delving into this kind of pricing strategy, you're not just collecting data; you're also paving the way for increased profits. The principle here is simple yet powerful: charge people based on their actual usage. This approach is particularly crucial in scenarios like a software company, where the number of users doesn't necessarily equate to a willingness to pay fivefold. This is where the art of bundling your services comes into play. It's about strategically creating categories beforehand, enabling you to guide customers into specific bundles that align with their needs and your pricing objectives.

Also, to measure how your marketing worked, you can calculate your net marketing contribution. It is a measure of marketing profitability that includes only components of profitability controlled by marketing.

NMC = net sales - cost of goods sold -marketing expenses

Now you need Marketing ROI, which is a measure of marketing productivity of a marketing investment.

Marketing ROI = [NMC] / [Marketing expenses]

As we wrap up this chapter on pricing, remember that the journey doesn't end here. Stay tuned for the next chapter, where we'll explore another facet of business strategy that's just as intriguing and essential. Get ready to dive deeper and keep the curiosity alive!

Pricing Strategy Development Table

When developing a pricing strategy, consider whether your prices are competitive, start with lower prices to gain market share, or set premium prices for exclusivity. It's also effective to initially set higher prices and gradually reduce them, offer a variety of price points, and account for extra costs like taxes and shipping. Clear payment terms are crucial for customer clarity. Remember, these strategies are guidelines and should be tailored to your specific market and business needs.

Strategy Component	Tactics to Implement	Initial Investment (₹)	Recurring Monthly Expenses (₹)
Market Research	Surveys, Data Analysis		
Competitive Analysis	Market Positioning Study		
Customer Profiling	Demographic Research		
Costing Analysis	Calculation of Production & Operational Costs		
Brand Development	Messaging, Identity Creation		
Pricing Structure	Tiered & Bundle Pricing Strategies		
Promotional Planning	Discount Strategies, Offers		
Logistics & Distribution	Channel Management, Logistics Planning		
Market Feedback Analysis	Consumer Response Studies		

Total Estimated Startup Marketing Costs | Initial Investment + Recurring Monthly Expenses (₹) |

Product Pricing Calculator

Units Produced per Hour:

Hourly Labor Cost: ₹

Total Cost per Unit: ₹ (Hourly Wage / # Units)

Material Cost per Unit: ₹

Overhead per Unit: ₹ (e.g., fees, advertising, packaging)

Total Production Cost: ₹ (Labor + Material + Overhead)

Desired Markup:

Final Product Price: ₹ (Total Cost x Markup)

Service Pricing Calculator

Hourly Rate for Service: ₹

Hours Required for Service:

Total Labor Cost for Service: ₹ (Hourly Rate x Hours)

Material Cost for Service: ₹

Service Overhead: ₹ (e.g., fees, advertising, travel)

Total Service Cost: ₹ (Labor + Material + Overhead)

Markup for Service:

Final Service Price: ₹ (Total Cost x Markup)

6.10 Analytics for Startups

"Success is not the key to happiness. Happiness is the key to success. If you love what you are doing, you will be successful."

– Albert Schweitzer

Would you like to be a person who has all the answers — or — The person who has the right questions?

It is practically impossible for any human to have all the answers…… am I correct?

I know you will agree with me. We all know that it is not about the path we choose, but it is about what actions we take.

Let's take the example of The BATMAN [The Dark Knight]

In this movie, Batman used the Sonar technology to monitor all incoming and outgoing calls.

In Christopher Nolan's "The Dark Knight" (2008), Batman's use of a unique sonar cell phone technology offers a compelling analogy to the world of analytics.

Just as Batman employs every cell phone in Gotham to create a real-time, 3D map of the city, businesses today harness vast amounts of data to gain insights and make informed decisions. However, the film also underscores a crucial lesson: the importance of human judgment in the realm of analytics.

Batman's sonar technology functions by transforming every cell phone into a sonar device. This high-frequency sonar pulse, similar to echolocation in bats, provides a detailed visualization of Gotham based on the echoes received from objects and people. In the realm of business analytics, this mirrors the process of collecting vast amounts of raw data, processing it, and using it to derive actionable insights.

Lucius Fox's was not happy…

But it highlights the film's central message: the importance of human oversight in decision-making.

While machines and algorithms can process vast amounts of data and provide insights, the human element evaluates the ethical ramifications and potential consequences of actions. In analytics, this translates to the need for human judgment in interpreting data, understanding its context, and making decisions that align with ethical standards.

In today's data-driven world, analytics plays a pivotal role in the success of any business, especially startups. With limited resources and a need to make every decision count, startups can leverage analytics to gain insights, make informed decisions, and drive growth.

From now on you will not have to search the internet and scorch the EARTH…

This guide delves deep into the importance of analytics, offering startups a comprehensive understanding and actionable strategies.

Analytics refers to the systematic computational analysis of data or statistics. It involves collecting, processing, and interpreting data to discover patterns and draw conclusions. Start by identifying the key data points relevant to your startup. This could be user behaviour, sales numbers, website traffic, etc.

Example:

Consider an e-commerce startup. Analytics can help determine which products are most popular, the average time users spend on the site, and the effectiveness of marketing campaigns.

Does this mean you have to rely on AI/ML to give you results?

- **The Challenge of Trusting Machines vs. Intuition:**
  - As advanced analytics evolve, managers often grapple with the decision of when to rely on data-driven insights and when to trust their instincts.

- **Human vs. Machine Decision-making:**
  - Humans excel in decisions involving intuition and ambiguity resolution.
  - Machines are superior in decisions requiring deduction, granularity, and scalability.

Which is better, Let find out, but first thing first. Understanding analytics and tools is important. After going through multiple articles, I can find out three types of analytics generally is there. But which one is better when to use and how much does it cost? I will give in a table below.

Criteria	Web Scraping	Surveys & Feedback Forms	Social Media Monitoring	Web Analytics	Public Datasets	IoT Devices & Sensors	Mobile Analytics
Description	Extracting data directly from websites.	Collecting data through questionnaires or feedback mechanisms.	Monitoring and analyzing data from social media platforms.	Analyzing user behavior and traffic on a website.	Accessing datasets made available to the public by organizations or governments.	Collecting data from physical devices in real-time.	Analyzing user behavior within mobile applications.
How to Do It	Use web scraping tools or write custom scripts.	Use online survey platforms or feedback tools.	Use social media analytics tools or platforms.	Use web analytics platforms or tools.	Search for relevant public datasets online.	Deploy sensors or IoT devices; collect and analyze data.	Use mobile analytics platforms or SDKs.
Relevance	Competitor analysis, market research, content aggregation.	Customer feedback, market research, product development.	Brand monitoring, sentiment analysis, market trends.	Understanding website performance and user behavior.	Research, market analysis, trend identification.	Real-world data collection, environment monitoring, user behavior.	Understanding app performance, user engagement, and retention.
Cost	Varies (free tools to premium).	Varies (free to premium plans).	Varies (free to premium plans).	Mostly free, premium features may cost.	Mostly free, some datasets may cost.	Varies based on device and platform.	Varies (free to premium plans).
Tools	Beautiful Soup, Scrapy, Octoparse, Import.io.	Google Forms, SurveyMonkey, Typeform, Qualtrics, JotForm.	Hootsuite, Brandwatch, Sprout Social, Mention, SocialBakers.	Google Analytics, Matomo, Mixpanel, Adobe Analytics.	Kaggle, Google Dataset Search, UCI ML Repository, AWS Public Datasets.	Arduino, Raspberry Pi, Particle, AWS IoT, Google Cloud IoT.	Firebase Analytics, Flurry, App Annie, Mixpanel, Localytics.
Pros	Direct access to data, customizable, can be automated.	Direct feedback, customizable, quantitative & qualitative data.	Real-time data, insights into sentiment, brand monitoring.	Detailed insights, user behavior, traffic sources.	Pre-collected, variety of topics, often cleaned.	Real-time data, versatile applications, integration capabilities.	Detailed insights, user segmentation, event tracking.
Cons	Legal concerns, websites can block, data may be unstructured.	Response bias, limited sample, time-consuming.	Data privacy, limited to public posts, platform restrictions.	Requires setup, data privacy concerns, cookie restrictions.	May be outdated, limited to available datasets, licensing restrictions.	Setup costs, data privacy, requires maintenance.	Platform restrictions, data privacy concerns, requires proper SDK integration.

For startups, begin with descriptive analytics to understand your current situation. As you grow, incorporate predictive and prescriptive analytics.

2. Why is Analytics Crucial for Startups?

Regularly review and analyze your data. Monthly or quarterly reviews can provide insights into trends and areas of improvement.

Insight into Customer Behavior:

Understanding customer preferences, habits, and pain points can help tailor products or services.

Data-Driven Decision Making:

Rather than relying on gut feelings, startups can make decisions based on concrete data.

Optimizing Marketing Efforts:

Determine which marketing channels are most effective and allocate resources accordingly.

4. Key Metrics Every Startup Should Track

Customer Acquisition Cost (CAC)

Lifetime Value (LTV)

Churn Rate

Conversion Rate

Net Promoter Score (NPS)

Use dashboards to visualize these metrics. Tools like Google Analytics or Tableau can provide real-time insights.

Best 8 questions you can ask to get the Best analysis

- What is the customer acquisition cost (CAC) for each marketing channel?

- What is the lifetime value (LTV) of our customers?

- Which marketing campaigns have the highest conversion rates?

- How do organic vs. paid campaigns perform in terms of leads and conversions?

- What times of day/week are most effective for our marketing efforts?

- How do different customer segments respond to our marketing campaigns?

- What is the bounce rate for our digital campaigns?

- How do offline and online marketing efforts complement each other?

Analytics is not just a buzzword; it's a necessity for startups in the modern business landscape. By understanding and leveraging analytics, startups can navigate the complexities of the business world and set themselves up for exponential growth.

Marketing analytics refers to the practice of measuring, managing, and analyzing marketing performance to maximize its effectiveness and optimize return on investment (ROI). It provides a detailed view of the performance of various marketing initiatives, allowing businesses to understand how their marketing activities are performing and where improvements can be made.

Google Shopping Insights Tutorial: How to analyze product searches

- Visit Google Shopping Insights.

- Enter the product or category you want to analyze.

- View search interest over time and by region.

- Compare against other products or categories.

- Gain insights into seasonal trends and consumer behaviour.

Do you want one more BONUS?

Well, I think you do, so I am giving you methods as a STARTUP owner you can use this method from the table to gather DATA. I know first roadblock for anything to get the data and how to get it.

Criteria	Descriptive Analytics	Predictive Analytics	Prescriptive Analytics
Definition	Focuses on understanding what happened in the past using historical data.	Uses machines to determine likely outcomes based on various input variables.	Machines make decisions based on defined objectives, analyzing large amounts of data, and running experiments to optimize outcomes.
Example	Monthly sales reports.	Sales forecasts.	Marketing strategies to increase sales.
Costs Required	Low to moderate (mainly data storage and basic analysis tools).	Moderate to high (advanced statistical tools, machine learning algorithms).	High (advanced analytics platforms, experimentation tools, decision optimization software).
Expertise	Basic data analysis skills.	Data science, machine learning, and statistical modeling expertise.	Advanced analytics, decision science, and domain-specific expertise.
Relevance	Relevant for all businesses to understand past performance.	Relevant for businesses looking to forecast future trends and outcomes.	Relevant for businesses looking to optimize decision-making and achieve specific objectives.
Stage of Business	All stages (especially for periodic reviews and audits).	Growth and maturity stages (when past data is available).	Maturity stage (when optimization is a key focus).
Data Required	Historical data.	Large amounts of historical data for accurate predictions.	Historical data, real-time data, and experimental data.
When is it Required?	Periodic reviews, end-of-month/quarter/year reports.	When forecasting future trends, budgeting, or planning for future scenarios.	When making strategic decisions, optimizing processes, or testing new strategies.
Human vs. AI	Primarily human-driven with support from basic analytics tools.	AI-driven (machine learning models) with human oversight for model training and validation.	AI-driven for analysis, but human judgment is crucial for implementing recommendations and understanding business implications.
Tools	Excel, Google Analytics, Tableau.	Python (libraries like Scikit-learn, TensorFlow), R, SAS, IBM SPSS.	IBM Decision Optimization, FICO Decision Management, Python (for custom solutions), A/B testing platforms like Optimizely or VWO.

6.11 Marketing Automation

"Opportunities don't happen, you create them."

– Chris Grosser

You want to create a TON of leads...... But you are busy doing work that does not require the MOST attention.

You should create a system that when you are sleeping your LEADS are being generated.

Yeah, analysis and stuff you need to do because of that you can manage your campaign, these days that also is assisted by AI

Who are YOU?? ...... you are Entrepreneur

What does an Entrepreneur do?? ...... They solve problems with their product

Do Entrepreneurs need to invest time in?? ...... Building right System

Yes, SYSTEM works and if you want to live a life more freely make sure people who are working for you know what they need to deliver. Similarly, if you can automate things through TOOLs, get it done.

Otherwise, you will have to go ROAD every day and as people to BUY your stuff [Well, that can be a part of marketing for the short term]

Marketing automation refers to the use of software and technology to automate repetitive marketing tasks, streamline marketing workflows, and measure outcomes. It's not just about efficiency; it's about enhancing the customer experience and driving more revenue.

Startups often run on limited resources. Automation helps in achieving more with less, reducing manual tasks and freeing up time for strategy and creativity.

As startups grow, the number of leads and customers can become overwhelming. Automation ensures that every lead is nurtured and no opportunity is missed.

Start by identifying high-value accounts. Use personalized content and targeted campaigns to engage these accounts.

Account-based marketing (ABM)

ABM is a strategy that targets high-value accounts instead of individual leads. It's about delivering personalized campaigns to engage each account, basing the marketing message on the specific attributes and needs of the account.

Examples: A SaaS company might target a large enterprise with personalized content that addresses the enterprise's specific pain points.

High-value leads.

Identify the best lead for a campaign or tactic. You can weigh important and undesirable behaviours automatically. By assigning values to leads based on their actions (like downloading a resource or visiting a pricing page), startups can prioritize high-value leads.

This involves tracking and managing prospective customers. It helps businesses understand which tactics are bringing in the best leads.

Examples: Using lead scoring to prioritize high-value leads.

Actionable Tips: Implement lead scoring. Use automation to nurture leads through the sales funnel.

It also pays off for your customers by solving common pain points that have arisen in the digital-first, omnichannel era

Most businesses consider marketing automation a middle-of-the-funnel tool, ideal for nurturing leads through automated email sequences

Multi-channel Campaigns:

Consumers interact with brands on multiple channels. Automation ensures consistent and coordinated messaging across all touchpoints.

CRM analytics

A seamless flow of data between marketing and sales ensures that leads don't fall through the cracks.

CRM analytics involves analyzing customer data to make informed business decisions. It provides insights into customer behaviour, sales trends, and marketing strategies.

Examples: Using CRM analytics to determine which products are most popular among a specific age group.

Regularly review CRM data. Use analytics tools to identify trends and patterns.

Setting Up Your Marketing Automation Strategy

Goal Setting: Whether it's increasing sales, boosting engagement, or reducing churn, define clear goals for your automation efforts.

Audience Segmentation: Not all customers are the same. Segment them based on behaviour, purchase history, or demographics to send targeted messages.

Content Mapping: Ensure that your content aligns with the buyer's journey. From awareness to consideration to decision, deliver relevant content at every stage.

Popular Marketing Automation Tools

HubSpot: A comprehensive tool offering everything from email automation to analytics. Ideal for startups looking for an all-in-one solution.

Marketo: With a focus on B2B, it offers robust lead management features.

Mailchimp: Beyond email, it now offers features like landing pages and ads.

ActiveCampaign: A powerful tool combining email marketing, automation, and CRM.

In the digital age, marketing automation is no longer a luxury; it's a necessity. For startups, it's the key to scaling efficiently, offering personalized experiences, and driving growth. With the right strategy and tools, any startup can harness the power of automation to achieve its goals.

7. Why do you need to connect Brand with Rituals?

"Act as if what you do makes a difference. It does."

– William James

This is interesting…

I know you have been following many rituals unknowingly, but you won't admit it.

In BRANDS case they make us practice this daily with products. It becomes such ingrained habits that we automatically lead to the sale of them.

What is your go-to place to EAT? …… Of Course, ZOMATO.

Rituals are an integral part of our life. WHY? Because it gives us a feeling of belonging. I have been brushing my teeth with the same toothpaste that I used to use when I was kid. Now, it has become a part of me.

Wherever I go I always try to find the same...... It actually makes me feel complete. Also, my teeth are clean with that.

Take a brand like Starbucks, for instance. You may start your day with a 'ritual' of grabbing a cup of their favorite Starbucks coffee. This ritualistic association elevates Starbucks from a mere coffee chain to a vital component of their morning routine.

I have got a clear IDEA now how to categorize the ritual formation. And I am more than happy to share a shortcut to share with you. So that you don't have to read multiple books.

This 3-stages was given by Arvind Sahay:

1. FIRST, Concept Formation:

In this stage, the product has to work with the BELIEFS of individuals. It involves getting introduced to the ideology and experience. This involves slow-decision making that matches the values of the brand and customer.

2. SECOND, Concept attainment:

Instead of slow-decision, it moved towards the medium decision based on brand concepts. Habits often start with a cue or trigger.

This could be a time of day, a particular feeling, or an event that prompts the user to turn to your product.

For example, if you're marketing a fitness app, the cue could be waking up in the morning, prompting the user to start their day with a quick workout. Identifying this cue is the first step to integrating your product into your user's daily routine

3. THIRD, Concept utilization:

It would be achieved when brand information has been successfully assimilated with fast and automatic retrieval. It's crucial to encourage repetition of the routine until it becomes a habit.

You can do this through reminders, providing regular positive reinforcement, and creating a community for users to share their experiences and successes. The goal is to make the routine so ingrained that the user feels a sense of incompleteness when they skip it.

Incorporating your brand into the rituals of your customers fosters a deeper sense of connection and loyalty. Rituals often evoke strong emotions, creating a bond between the brand and the customer. This emotional connection can lead to increased customer retention and brand loyalty, which are vital for business growth.

In an increasingly competitive market, connecting your brand with rituals can be a game-changer. Rituals offer familiarity and comfort to customers, helping to deepen emotional connections, foster loyalty, and boost engagement.

By integrating your brand into your customers' rituals, you're not just selling a product or service - you're becoming a part of their lives.

Navigating the world of marketing can sometimes feel daunting, but remember, you're not alone. We've seen firsthand how introducing rituals into a brand strategy can completely transform the relationship between a company and its customers.

8. Learnings from Superfans – Creating FANS of your Product

"With the new day comes new strength and new thoughts."

– Eleanor Roosevelt

Imagine strolling through the bustling streets of Indore, where you come across a unique tea joint, Chai Sutta Bar. Known for its traditional yet modern approach, this cafe serves chai in earthen kulhads, evoking nostalgia and a sense of cultural connection. It's more than just a tea spot; it's a hangout for the young and old, symbolizing the blend of tradition and contemporary trends in India.

This example illustrates the essence of audience building in India's diverse cultural landscape. By tapping into familiar traditions and marrying them with modern elements, Chai Sutta Bar has created a space that resonates deeply with the Indian audience. This story sets the stage for understanding how to connect with and build a dedicated audience in the dynamic, multifaceted Indian market.

Understanding this landscape is crucial for anyone looking to establish a foothold in the Indian market. Whether it's a local startup or an international brand, the key lies in embracing this diversity, tailoring approaches to resonate with different cultural nuances, and building relationships based on trust and understanding. This chapter delves into how to successfully build and engage an audience in India's multifaceted market.

- **Engage Your Audience:** Use storytelling to connect with your audience. Share stories that resonate with Indian culture and values. Engage them with content that reflects their interests and preferences. Leverage popular Indian festivals, events, and trends to make your content more relatable.

- **Foster Interaction:** Encourage active participation. Create interactive content like polls, quizzes, and contests that are culturally relevant. Use social media platforms popular in India to host live sessions, AMAs (Ask Me Anything), and discussions that encourage audience interaction.

- **Break the Ice:** This is about making your audience feel comfortable and welcomed. Start conversations on social media with topics that are familiar and engaging to the Indian audience. Host virtual meet-and-greets or community events that resonate with local interests.

- **Personalized Communication:** Tailor your communication to reflect the diverse cultures within India. Use regional languages where appropriate and acknowledge local festivals and celebrations. Personalized emails or messages that cater to individual preferences can significantly enhance audience engagement.

- **Unique Experiences:** Offer experiences or products that are exclusive to the Indian market. This could be in the form of early access to new products, India-specific promotions, or events that celebrate Indian culture and traditions.

- **Build Community:** Create a sense of community among your audience. Encourage them to share their experiences and stories. Build platforms, like forums or social media groups, where they can connect over shared interests or localities.

- **Address Challenges:** Understand and navigate the diverse linguistic, cultural, and regional preferences in India. Be adaptable in your approach and sensitive to the varying needs and expectations of different Indian audiences.

- **Value Your Audience:** Show genuine appreciation for your audience. Highlight customer stories, respond to feedback, and engage regularly. Organize customer appreciation events or loyalty programs that resonate with Indian consumers.

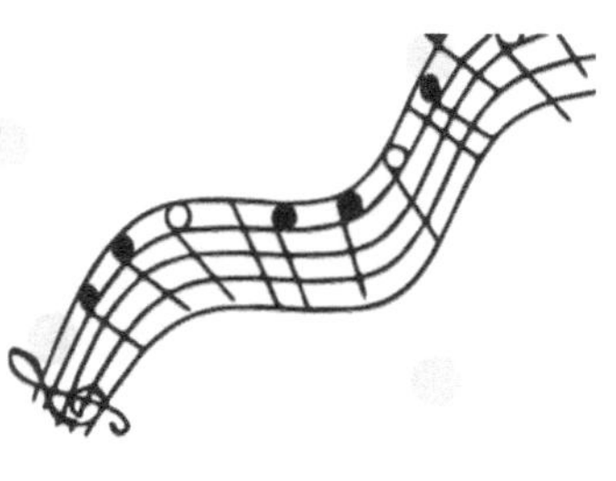

PITCHING

9. Pitch

"Today's accomplishments were yesterday's impossibilities."

– Robert H. Schuller

In the bustling world of Indian business, where ideas clash and innovations compete for attention, mastering the art of the pitch is crucial. Whether you're a dentist in Mumbai or a startup founder in Bengaluru, the skill to convincingly present your ideas can be the difference between success and obscurity. This need stems from a fundamental gap between our intentions and how others perceive them, a gap deeply rooted in the evolution of the human brain.

Understanding the Brain's Evolution in Pitching:

The brain, a complex organ, evolved in stages, each adding a layer to our cognitive abilities. First, there's the 'croc brain,' primitive and focused on survival. It reacts emotionally and simplistically, filtering out anything not immediately striking. Next is the midbrain, responsible for processing social cues and more complex scenarios. Finally, the neocortex, the seat of logic and analysis, evolved. When pitching, we use our neocortex, but our audience first processes it with their 'croc brain.' Thus, your pitch must be simple, clear, and compelling enough to pass this initial filter.

Creating Desire and Tension:

Imagine you're pitching to a potential investor in Delhi's dynamic market. The key is to grab and retain their attention, achieved by triggering desire and tension. Desire is kindled by offering a tantalizing reward – perhaps the promise of tapping into India's vast consumer market. Tension, however, is created by the fear of loss – missing out on a lucrative opportunity. This psychological play stimulates neurotransmitters in the brain, making your pitch more impactful.

Frame Control:

In any meeting, each participant views the situation through their own 'frame' – a mix of beliefs, experiences, and values. The dominant frame dictates the flow of the meeting. For instance, a customer might see the price as paramount, while you stress on quality. Gaining frame control means your perspective becomes the guiding narrative. If you're pitching eco-friendly packaging to a Chennai-based company, and you manage to make sustainability the dominant frame, you've gained an upper hand.

Countering Common Frames:

Be prepared to counter typical frames in business pitches. The power frame, often exuding arrogance, must be met with defiance, ensuring your idea isn't overshadowed. The time frame, where the client controls the timing, can be countered by showing you're equally in command of your schedule. The analyst frame, bogged down in details, should be met with high-level responses, focusing the conversation back on the bigger picture.

Prizing Yourself:

In the Indian market, where competition is fierce, position yourself or your product as the prize. This reverses the dynamic, making the client or investor seek your approval. Take inspiration from exclusive brands that make customers aspire to qualify for their products.

Triggering Hot Cognitions:

Decisions are often made instinctively. After establishing your pitch's core idea, aim to trigger these 'hot cognitions.' This involves stacking multiple frames – an intriguing narrative, a prize frame making them qualify for your opportunity, and a time frame adding urgency. This approach can quickly turn a skeptical listener into an eager participant.

Avoiding Neediness:

Nothing undermines a pitch more than desperation. Conveying a lack of need, showcasing your strengths, and occasionally withdrawing, can make your target pursue you, rather than the other way around. This is particularly effective in a culture that respects self-assuredness and confidence.

Attaining Situational Alpha Status:

In Indian society, where hierarchical dynamics often play out, attaining situational alpha status in a meeting is vital. This involves asserting your expertise and steering the conversation to areas where you are the authority. Avoid falling into beta traps, like being made to wait unnecessarily.

Keeping It Short and Simple:

Your pitch should be concise and straightforward. Begin by establishing credibility, address why now is the opportune moment for your idea, and succinctly present your big idea, focusing on how it fills a market gap or addresses a specific need.

In the Indian context, where market dynamics are rapidly evolving, these strategies from 'Pitch Anything' can be transformative. Understanding the psychological underpinnings of a successful pitch, tailoring your approach to the Indian market's nuances, and presenting your ideas with confidence and clarity can significantly increase your chances of success.

9.1 Tactics to optimize your Deal

Creating a conversational and accessible summary of "The Psychology of Negotiation: A Checklist of" by Nick Kolenda, we'll delve into the key strategies for optimizing deals, integrating the latest statistics and practical insights where relevant.

Welcome to an exciting and pivotal chapter in "Zero to Everyone," where we delve deep into the art of effective advertisement, specifically tailored for Indian entrepreneurs. This journey is about more than just creating ads; it's about connecting, influencing, and engaging with a diverse and dynamic audience. Here, I'll share with you a plethora of strategies, insights, and tips, all designed to elevate your advertising game in India's unique market.

The Preliminaries: Setting the Stage for Success

Let's start with the groundwork. Before you even begin to design your ad, it's crucial to understand the landscape. Research your competitors, understand market rates, and know what deals you deserve. It's like preparing for a crucial exam – the more you know, the stronger your position. Enhance your BATNAs (Best Alternatives to a Negotiated Agreement). For instance, if you're a job seeker, explore multiple opportunities. This approach boosts your negotiation power by ensuring you have options.

Negotiate when the weather is nice – it might sound quirky, but sunny days tend to uplift moods, leading to more positive interactions. Also, aim for morning negotiations. The early hours are golden for clear thinking and decision-making, plus being first in line can work in your favor due to the 'primacy effect'.

During the Negotiation: The Dance of Persuasion

Now, let's talk about the negotiation itself. Build rapport by sharing personal stories and bring pastries and coffee to the table. This not only builds a rapport but also triggers reciprocity. Frame your sales as training information to avoid triggering defensive reactions.

Be mindful of body language and perceived power dynamics. For instance, providing a low soft chair for your counterpart can subtly influence the negotiation in your favor. Mention your alternatives transparently to make negotiations more effective. Stay firm and confident in your language and avoid weak phrases that undermine your position.

Show emotions like anger and disappointment sparingly; these can lead to larger concessions but must be used judiciously. Don't fixate on one aspect of the negotiation, like salary in job negotiations – consider other benefits too. Breaking down benefits makes them feel more substantial, and depicting visual balance in offers ensures no party feels undervalued.

Make the first offer to set a high anchor, and when providing ranges, be specific rather than round. Simple contingencies in offers can facilitate agreement, and a pause after an offer can sometimes lead your counterpart to enhance their offer.

The Aftermath: Sealing the Deal

Post-negotiation, aim to be the first to draft the contract. This allows you to shape the terms more favorably. It's a critical step in ensuring that the agreement reflects your interests and the negotiation's outcome.

Negotiation is an art blended with science. These tactics, peppered with a dash of psychology, can significantly improve your negotiation outcomes. Remember, it's not just about winning but creating a win-win scenario!

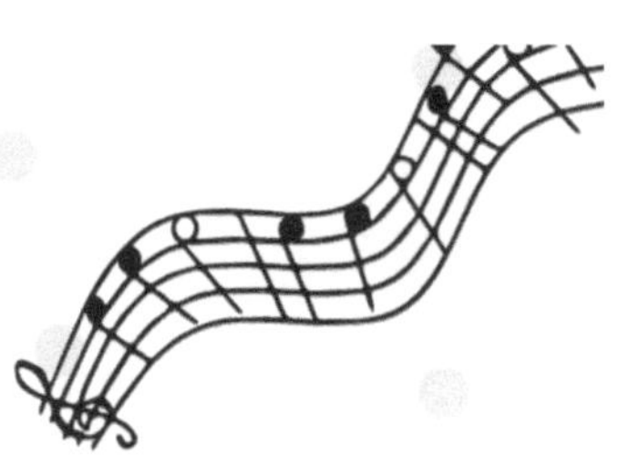

PR

10. Managing Public Relations and Image Building

"Your personal brand is a promise to your clients… a promise of quality, consistency, competency, and reliability."

– Jason Hartman

Public relations (PR) is an essential tool for any entrepreneur looking to grow their business. It's not just about managing the flow of information between an organization and the public; it's a strategic communication process that builds mutually beneficial relationships. In today's competitive market, understanding and effectively managing public relations can make the difference between thriving and merely surviving.

Understanding Public Relations

Public relations is much more than just publicity. It encompasses a range of strategies and techniques used to **convey the right message to the right audience**, build relationships, and create a positive image for your business. It's about storytelling – crafting and spreading your company's narrative in a way that resonates with your audience.

Image Building: The Core of PR

Your business's image is how the public perceives you. It's a combination of your identity, your communications, and the public's response to these. Building a positive image is a meticulous process that requires consistency, clarity, and authenticity. Remember, a strong image aligns with your business values and communicates them clearly to your audience.

Strategies for Effective Public Relations

- **Know Your Audience:** Understanding your audience is key. Tailor your message to resonate with them. Who are they? What do they care about? How do they prefer to receive information?

- **Crafting Your Message:** Your message should be clear, consistent, and true to your brand. It should reflect your business values and resonate with your audience's beliefs and needs.

- **Media Relations:** Building a good relationship with the media is crucial. They are your gateway to the public. Understand their needs and interests, and provide them with valuable, newsworthy stories.

- **Digital PR Strategies:** In the digital age, online presence is vital. Use social media, blogs, and your website to communicate directly with your audience. Engage with them, listen to their feedback, and participate in the online community.

- **Crisis Management:** Always be prepared for a crisis. Have a crisis communication plan in place. In times of trouble, communicate openly, honestly, and promptly to maintain trust.

- **Measuring Success:** Evaluate your PR efforts. Are you reaching your target audience? Is your message being received as intended? Use tools like surveys, website analytics, and media coverage analysis to measure the impact of your PR strategies.

Myntra, an online fashion retailer in India, has successfully used public relations strategies to enhance its market presence. One notable example is Myntra's "End of Reason Sale" campaign. This campaign utilized a mix of social media buzz, celebrity endorsements, and strategic partnerships to generate excitement and engagement among consumers. By leveraging the power of influencers and creating an event-like atmosphere around their sales, Myntra effectively drove traffic and sales, while also solidifying its position as a trendy and accessible fashion destination in the Indian market.

Applying the earlier mentioned PR steps to Myntra's strategy:

- **Know Your Audience:** Myntra targeted young, fashion-conscious consumers in India, understanding their preferences for trendy, affordable fashion.

- **Crafting Your Message:** The campaign's message was about offering high fashion at great discounts, positioning Myntra as a go-to destination for fashion deals.

- **Media Relations:** Myntra leveraged media platforms, especially social media, to spread the word about their sale, using influencer marketing and digital advertising.

- **Digital PR Strategies:** They created a buzz on social media with hashtags, influencer collaborations, and teasers about the sale.

- **Crisis Management:** While not specifically applicable in this example, Myntra maintains a responsive customer service to handle any issues, maintaining their brand reputation.

- **Measuring Success:** Myntra tracked the success of their campaign through increased website traffic, sales figures, and social media engagement metrics.

For entrepreneurs, managing public relations and building a positive image is not just about selling a product or service; it's about building trust, establishing credibility, and forging lasting relationships with your audience. In the journey from zero to market leader, effective public relations is your most powerful ally.

Bibliography

Aaker, David A. Building Strong Brands. Simon and Schuster, 2012.

Brunson, Russell. Dotcom Secrets. Hay House, Inc, 2020.

---. Expert Secrets. Hay House, Inc, 2022.

---. Traffic Secrets. Hay House, Inc, 2023.

Cardone, Grant. The 10X Rule. John Wiley & Sons, 2011.

Cialdini, Robert. Pre-Suasion. Simon and Schuster, 2016.

Drummond, Graeme, et al. Strategic Marketing. Routledge, 2010.

Edwards, Jim. Copywriting Secrets. 2019.

Eyal, Nir. Hooked. Penguin, 2014.

Flynn, Pat. Superfans. Get Smart Books, 2019.

Gladwell, Malcolm. The Tipping Point. Little, Brown, 2006.

Godin, Seth. This Is Marketing. Portfolio, 2018.

Greene, Robert. The 48 Laws of Power. Penguin, 2000.

Hopkins, Claude. Scientific Advertising. Sound Wisdom, 2023.

Kaufman, Josh. The Personal MBA. Penguin UK, 2012.

Keller, Gary, and Jay Papasan. The ONE Thing. Bard Press, 2013.

Klaff, Oren. Pitch Anything: An Innovative Method for Presenting, Persuading, and Winning the Deal. McGraw Hill Professional, 2011.

Kotler, Philip, et al. Principles of Marketing. Pearson UK, 2019.

Lindstrom, Martin. Buyology. Currency, 2010.

Miller, Donald. Building a StoryBrand. HarperCollins Leadership, 2017.

Ogilvy, David. Ogilvy on Advertising. Vintage, 2013.

PhD, Robert B. Cialdini. Influence, New and Expanded. HarperCollins, 2021.

Rajamannar, Raja. Quantum Marketing. HarperCollins Leadership, 2021.

Renvoise, Patrick, and Christophe Morin. Neuromarketing. HarperCollins Leadership, 2007.

Ries, Al, and Laura Ries. The 22 Immutable Laws of Branding. Harper Collins, 2009.

Sahay, Arvind. Brands And The Brain. Penguin Random House India Private Limited, 2022.

Scott, David Meerman. The New Rules of Marketing and PR. John Wiley & Sons, 2015.

Sharp. How Brands Grow. OUP Australia & New Zealand, 2010.

Underhill, Paco. Why We Buy. 1999.

PickyStory. (n.d.). Post-Purchase Dissonance: Ways to Reduce Post-Purchase Dissonance with Examples. Retrieved from https://pickystory.com/blog/post-purchase-dissonance-ways-to-reduce-post-purchase-dissonance-with-examples/

Ambitions Behavioral Health. (n.d.). Average Human Attention Span Statistics. Retrieved from https://www.ambitionsaba.com/resources/average-human-attention-span-statistics

Roberts, D. L. (n.d.). Cognitive Bias Part 1: What They Are & What They Do. Newsbreak Original. Retrieved from https://original.newsbreak.com/@dr-donna-l-roberts-561947/2648420901263-cognitive-bias-part-1-what-they-are-what-they-do

De Francisco, E. (n.d.). How to Sell to the Brain. Retrieved from https://www.elenadefrancisco.com/how-to-sell-to-the-brain/#:~:text=These%20are%20the%20ways%20to,and%20playing%20an%20emotional%20chord.

Soula, L. (n.d.). Understanding Six Stimuli that Influence the Primal Brain. LinkedIn. Retrieved from https://www.linkedin.com/pulse/understanding-six-stimuli-influence-primal-brain-personal-soula/

Author(s) Unknown. (n.d.). [Title of the Article]. ScienceDirect. Retrieved from https://www.sciencedirect.com/science/article/abs/pii/B9780123970251001561

Garrison, K. E., & Knight, R. T. (2015). The Neuroscience of Natural Rewards: Relevance to Addictive Drugs. Journal of Neuroscience, 35(19), 7236-7245. Retrieved from https://www.ncbi.nlm.nih.gov/pmc/articles/PMC4406946/

Dooley, R. (2019, January). Neuromarketing: What You Need to Know. Harvard Business Review. Retrieved from https://hbr.org/2019/01/neuromarketing-what-you-need-to-know

Author(s) Unknown. (n.d.). [Title of the Article]. NeurosciRN. Retrieved from https://neuroscirn.org/v3i4a58/

Author(s) Unknown. (2004). [Title of the Article]. Neuron. Retrieved from https://www.cell.com/neuron/fulltext/S0896-6273(04)00612-9?_return URL=https%3A%2F%2Flinkinghub.elsevier.com%2Fretrieve%2Fpii%2FS0896627304006129%3Fshowall%3Dtrue

Garrison, K. E., & Knight, R. T. (2021). The Neuroscience of Reward and Decision Making. Journal of Neuroscience, 41(5), 930-938. Retrieved from https://ncbi.nlm.nih.gov/pmc/articles/PMC7856827/

World Health Organization Europe. (n.d.). Encouraging Health Warnings on Tobacco Packaging. Retrieved from https://who.int/europe/activities/encouraging-health-warnings-on-tobacco-packaging

Performance Marketing World. (n.d.). Gender Shopping Gap: Men Spend 75% More on Goods Bought In-Store. Retrieved from https://www.performancemarketingworld.com/article/1751425/gender-shopping-gap-men-spend-75-goods-bought-in-store

Charged Retail. (2022, March 9). Shopping Habits Among Men and Women Are Widening, According to Study. Retrieved from https://www.chargedretail.co.uk/2022/03/09/shopping-habits-among-men-and-women-are-widening-according-to-study/

FinanceBuzz. (n.d.). Male vs. Female Spending Statistics. Retrieved from https://financebuzz.com/male-vs-female-spending-statistics

Adglow. (n.d.). E-commerce: Men Spend More Than Women. Retrieved from https://www.adglow.com/en-us/blog/pt-br/e-commerce-men-spend-more-than-women

SageSeller. (n.d.). Difference Between Men and Women Shopping Behaviors. Retrieved from https://sageseller.com/blog/difference-between-men-and-women-shopping-behaviors/

Knowledge@Wharton. (n.d.). Men Buy, Women Shop: The Sexes Have Different Priorities When Walking Down the Aisles. Retrieved from https://knowledge.wharton.upenn.edu/podcast/knowledge-at-wharton-podcast/men-buy-women-shop-the-sexes-have-different-priorities-when-walking-down-the-aisles/

Times of India. (n.d.). Differences in Shopping Habits Between Men and Women. Retrieved from https://timesofindia.indiatimes.com/life-style/fashion/buzz/differences-in-shopping-habits-between-men-and-women/articleshow/87263287.cms

OnlineDasher. (n.d.). Male vs. Female Shopping Statistics. Retrieved from https://www.onlinedasher.com/male-vs-female-shopping-statistics/

Capital One Shopping. (n.d.). Male vs. Female Shopping Statistics. Retrieved from https://capitaloneshopping.com/research/male-vs-female-shopping-statistics/

Worldometer. (n.d.). India Demographics. Retrieved from https://www.worldometers.info/demographics/india-demographics/

Ariely, D. (2008). Predictably Irrational: The Hidden Forces That Shape Our Decisions. New York, NY: HarperCollins

Baron, J. (2007). Thinking and Deciding (4th ed.). New York, NY: Cambridge University Press.

Bless, H., Fiedler, K., & Strack, F. (2004). Social cognition: How individuals construct social reality. Hove and New York: Psychology Press.

Gonzalez, C. (2017). Decision-making: A cognitive science perspective. In S. Chipman (Ed.), The Oxford handbook of cognitive science (pp. 249–264). Oxford University Press. Accessed on July 9, 2020 from https://www.cmu.edu/dietrich/sds/ddmlab/papers/oxfordhb-9780199842193-e-6.pdf

Haselton, M. G., Nettle, D., & Andrews, P. W. (2005). The evolution of cognitive bias. In Buss DM (ed.). The Handbook of Evolutionary Psychology. Hoboken, NJ, US: John Wiley & Sons Inc. pp. 724–746.

Kahneman, D. (2011). Thinking, fast and slow. Farrar, Straus, and Giroux.

Kahneman, D., & Frederick, S. (2002). Representativeness Revisited: Attribute Substitution in Intuitive Judgment. In Gilovich T, Griffin DW, Kahneman D (eds.). Heuristics and Biases: The Psychology of Intuitive Judgment. Cambridge: Cambridge University Press. pp. 51–52

Morewedge, C. K., & Kahneman, D. (October 2010). Associative processes in intuitive judgment. Trends in Cognitive Sciences,14(10): 435–40. doi:10.1016/j.tics.2010.07.004

Tversky, A., & Kahneman, D. (1974). Judgment under uncertainty: Heuristics and biases. Science, 185, 1124–1131.

Briesch, R. A., Krishnamurthi, L., Mazumdar, T., & Raj, S. P. (1997).

A comparative analysis of reference price models. Journal of

Consumer Research, 24(2), 202-214.

Mazumdar, T., Raj, S. P., & Sinha, I. (2005). Reference price research:

Review and propositions. Journal of marketing, 69(4), 84-102.

Briesch, R. A., Krishnamurthi, L., Mazumdar, T., & Raj, S. P. (1997). "A comparative analysis of reference price models." Journal of Consumer Research, 24(2), 202-214.

Mazumdar, T., Raj, S. P., & Sinha, I. (2005). "Reference price research: Review and propositions." Journal of Marketing, 69(4), 84-102.

Coulter, K. S., & Coulter, R. A. (2005). "Size does matter: The effects of magnitude representation congruency on price perceptions and purchase likelihood." Journal of Consumer Psychology, 15(1), 64-76.

Deng, X., & Kahn, B. E. (2009). "Is your product on the right side? The "location effect" on perceived product heaviness and package evaluation." Journal of Marketing Research, 46(6), 725-738.

Coulter, K. S., Choi, P., & Monroe, K. B. (2012). "Comma N'cents in pricing: The effects of auditory representation encoding on price magnitude perceptions." Journal of Consumer Psychology, 22(3), 395-407.

Davis, D. F., Bagchi, R., & Block, L. G. (2016). "Alliteration alters: Phonetic overlap in promotional messages influences evaluations and choice." Journal of Retailing, 92(1), 1-12.

Baroody, A. J. (1985). "Mastery of basic number combinations: Internalization of relationships or facts?" Journal for Research in Mathematics Education, 16(2), 83-98.

King, D., & Janiszewski, C. (2011). "The sources and consequences of the fluent processing of numbers." Journal of Marketing Research, 48(2), 327-341.

Puccinelli, N. M., Chandrashekaran, R., Grewal, D., & Suri, R. (2013). "Are men seduced by red? The effect of red versus black prices on price perceptions." Journal of Retailing, 89(2), 115-125.

Yang, S. S., Kimes, S. E., & Sessarego, M. M. (2009). "Menu price presentation influences on consumer purchase behavior in restaurants." International Journal of Hospitality Management, 28(1), 157-160.

Adaval, R., & Monroe, K. B. (2002). "Automatic construction and use of contextual information for product and price evaluations." Journal of Consumer Research, 28(4), 572-588.

Nunes, J. C., & Boatwright, P. (2004). "Incidental prices and their effect on willingness to pay." Journal of Marketing Research, 41(4), 457-466.

Bagchi, R., & Davis, D. F. (2012). "29 for 70 items or 70 items for 29? How presentation order affects package perceptions." Journal of Consumer Research, 39(1), 62-73.

Suk, K., Lee, J., & Lichtenstein, D. R. (2012). "The influence of price presentation order on consumer choice." Journal of Marketing Research, 49(5), 708-717.

Mogilner, C., & Aaker, J. (2009). "The time vs. money effect: Shifting product attitudes and decisions through personal connection." Journal of Consumer Research, 36(2), 277-291.

Chloe, Y., & Kan, C. (2021). "Budget depreciation: when budgeting early increases spending." Journal of Consumer Research, 47(6), 937-958.

Lee, C. Y., & Morewedge, C. K. (2023). "Mental accounting of product returns." Journal of Consumer Psychology.

Thomas, M., & Morwitz, V. (2005). "Penny wise and pound foolish: the left-digit effect in price cognition." Journal of Consumer Research, 32(1), 54-64.

Dehaene, S. (1992). "Varieties of numerical abilities." Cognition, 44(1-2), 1-42.

Morwitz, V. G., Greenleaf, E. A., & Johnson, E. J. (1998). "Divide and prosper: consumers' reactions to partitioned prices." Journal of Marketing Research, 35(4), 453-463.

Thomas, M., Simon, D. H., & Kadiyali, V. (2007). "Do consumers perceive precise prices to be lower than round prices? Evidence from laboratory and market data." Johnson School at Cornell University Research Paper, (09-07).

Coulter, K. S. (2007). "The effects of digit-direction on eye movement bias and price- rounding behavior." Journal of Product & Brand Management.

Pelham, B. W., Carvallo, M., & Jones, J. T. (2005). "Implicit egotism." Current Directions in Psychological Science, 14(2), 106-110.

Wadhwa, M., & Zhang, K. (2015). "This number just feels right: The impact of roundedness of price numbers on product evaluations." Journal of Consumer Research, 41(5), 1172-1185.

Kim, J., Malkoc, S. A., & Goodman, J. K. (2022). "The threshold-crossing effect: Just-below pricing discourages consumers to upgrade." Journal of Consumer Research, 48(6), 1096-1112.

Coulter, K. S., & Norberg, P. A. (2009). "The effects of physical distance between regular and sale prices on numerical difference perceptions." Journal of Consumer Psychology, 19(2), 144-157.

Feng, S., Suri, R., Chao, M. C. H., & Koc, U. (2017). "Presenting comparative price promotions vertically or horizontally: Does it matter?" Journal of Business Research, 76, 209-218.

Hung, H. H., Cheng, Y. H., Chuang, S. C., Yu, A. P. I., & Lin, Y. T. (2021). "Consistent price endings increase consumers perceptions of cheapness." Journal of Retailing and Consumer Services, 61, 102590.

Korvorst, M., & Damian, M. F. (2008). "The differential influence of decades and units on multidigit number comparison." Quarterly Journal of Experimental Psychology, 61(8), 1250-1264.

Coulter, K. S., & Coulter, R. A. (2007). "Distortion of price discount perceptions: The right digit effect." Journal of Consumer Research, 34(2), 162-173.

González, E. M., Esteva, E., Roggeveen, A. L., & Grewal, D. (2016). "Amount off versus percentage off—when does it matter?" Journal of Business Research, 69(3), 1022-1027.

Guha, A., Biswas, A., Grewal, D., Verma, S., Banerjee, S., & Nordfält, J. (2018). "Reframing the discount as a comparison against the sale price: does it make the discount more attractive?" Journal of Marketing Research, 55(3), 339-351.

Mazumdar, T., Raj, S. P., & Sinha, I. (2005). "Reference price research: Review and propositions." Journal of Marketing, 69(4), 84-102.

Gourville, J. T. (1998). "Pennies-a-day: The effect of temporal reframing on transaction evaluation." Journal of Consumer Research, 24(4), 395-408.

Gourville, J. T. (1999). "The effect of implicit versus explicit comparisons on temporal pricing claims." Marketing Letters, 10(2), 113-124.

Gourville, J. T. (2003). "The effects of monetary magnitude and level of aggregation on the temporal framing of price." Marketing Letters, 14, 125-135.

Brough, A. R., & Chernev, A. (2012). "When opposites detract: Categorical reasoning and subtractive valuations of product combinations." Journal of Consumer Research, 39(2), 399-414.

Nunes, J. C., & Park, C. W. (2003). "Incommensurate resources: Not just more of the same." Journal of Marketing

DataReportal. (2023). Global Digital Overview. Retrieved from https://datareportal.com/global-digital-overview

Statista. (2023). Social Media Advertising Worldwide. Retrieved from https://www.statista.com/outlook/dmo/digital-advertising/social-media-advertising/worldwide

Data.ai. (2023). State of App Revenue 2023. Retrieved from https://www.data.ai/en/insights/market-data/state-of-app-revenue-2023/

Google. YouTube Mobile Advertising Statistics. Retrieved from https://www.thinkwithgoogle.com/marketing-strategies/app-and-mobile/youtube-mobile-advertising-statistics/

Khoros. (2022). Social Media Demographics Guide. Retrieved from https://khoros.com/resources/social-media-demographics-guide

Interactive Advertising Bureau (IAB). (2023). Internet Advertising Revenue Report 2022. Retrieved from https://www.iab.com/wp-content/uploads/2023/04/IAB_PwC_Internet_Advertising_Revenue_Report_2022.pdf

Insider Intelligence. (2022). US Social Buyers Spending More Than Ever. Retrieved from https://www.insiderintelligence.com/content/us-social-buyers-spending-more-than-ever

GlobalWebIndex/DataReportal. (2023). Social Media Users. Retrieved from https://datareportal.com/social-media-users

TikTok. (March 2023). 150 Million US Users. Retrieved from https://newsroom.tiktok.com/en-us/150-m-us-users

Meta. (2022). Meta Q2 2022 Earnings Call Transcript. Retrieved from https://s21.q4cdn.com/399680738/files/doc_financials/2022/q2/Meta-Q2-2022-Earnings-Call-Transcript.pdf

ShopPop. Click-to-Message Feature. Retrieved from https://shoppop.com/

Instagram. (2023). Getting Started with Instagram Business. Retrieved from https://business.instagram.com/getting-started

Statista. (2023). Instagram Global Age Group. Retrieved from https://www.statista.com/statistics/325587/instagram-global-age-group/

We Are Social. (2022). The Global State of Digital in July. Retrieved from https://wearesocial.com/uk/blog/2022/07/the-global-state-of-digital-in-july-part-two/

Snapchat. (2022). Why Snapchat Ads. Retrieved from https://forbusiness.snapchat.com/advertising/why-snapchat-ads

Snapchat/Neuro-Insight. (2022). Happy Emotions Drive Deeper Engagements. Retrieved from https://forbusiness.snapchat.com/blog/happy-emotions-drive-deeper-engagements

LinkedIn. (2023). LinkedIn Ads. Retrieved from https://business.linkedin.com/marketing-solutions/ads

Biteable. (2021). Video Marketing Statistics. Retrieved from https://biteable.com/blog/video-marketing-statistics/

Insider Intelligence. (2022 & 2023). Ad Costs Narrowing on Major Streaming Platforms. Retrieved from https://www.insiderintelligence.com/content/ad-costs-narrowing-on-major-streaming-platforms

Kolenda, Nick. "The Psychology of Advertising: How to Optimize the Text, Imagery, and Framing of Ads." NickKolenda.com. 2015, 2023.

Bourne, V. J. (2006). "The divided visual field paradigm: Methodological considerations." Laterality, 11(4), 373-393.

Grobelny, J., & Michalski, R. (2015). "The role of background color, interletter spacing, and font size on preferences in the digital presentation of a product." Computers in Human Behavior, 43, 85-100.

Meyers-Levy, J., & Peracchio, L. A. (1995). "Understanding the effects of color: How the correspondence between available and required resources affects attitudes." Journal of Consumer Research, 22(2), 121-138.

Pieters, R., & Wedel, M. (2004). "Attention capture and transfer in advertising: Brand, pictorial, and text-size effects." Journal of Marketing, 68(2), 36-50.

Shapiro, S. A., & Nielsen, J. H. (2013). "What the blind eye sees: Incidental change detection as a source of perceptual fluency." Journal of Consumer Research, 39(6), 1202-1218.

Chandy, R. K., Tellis, G. J., MacInnis, D. J., & Thaivanich, P. (2001). "What to say when: Advertising appeals in evolving markets." Journal of Marketing Research, 38(4), 399-414.

Lee, A. Y., & Labroo, A. A. (2004). "The effect of conceptual and perceptual fluency on brand evaluation." Journal of Marketing Research, 41(2), 151-165.

Sahni, N. S. (2015). "Effect of temporal spacing between advertising exposures: Evidence from online field experiments." Quantitative Marketing and Economics, 13(3), 203-247.

[Additional Indian Market Specific Sources] - This would include any references to Indian market trends, consumer behavior studies, cultural insights, or statistical data relevant to the Indian context.

Monnier, A., & Thomas, M. (2022). Experiential and Analytical Price Evaluations: How Experiential Product Description Affects Prices. Journal of Consumer Research.

Johnson, E. J., Hershey, J., Meszaros, J., & Kunreuther, H. (1993). Framing, probability distortions, and insurance decisions. Journal of Risk and Uncertainty, 7(1), 35-51.

Hadjichristidis, C., Handley, S. J., Sloman, S. A., Evans, J. S. B., Over, D. E., & Stevenson, R. J. (2007). Iffy beliefs: Conditional thinking and belief change. Memory & Cognition, 35(8), 2052-2059.

Jacoby, J., Nelson, M. C., & Hoyer, W. D. (1982). Corrective advertising and affirmative disclosure statements: Their potential for confusing and misleading the consumer.

Journal of Marketing, 46(1), 61-72.

Collins, A. M., & Loftus, E. F. (1975). A spreading-activation theory of semantic processing. Psychological Review, 82(6), 407.

Alter, A. L., & Oppenheimer, D. M. (2009). Uniting the tribes of fluency to form a metacognitive nation. Personality and Social Psychology Review, 13(3), 219-235.

Ehrlich, K., & Johnson-Laird, P. N. (1982). Spatial descriptions and referential continuity. Journal of Verbal Learning and Verbal Behavior, 21(3), 296-306.

Kamalski, J. (2007). Coherence Marking, Comprehension and Persuasion on the processing and representations of discourse. Doctoral dissertation, Netherlands Graduate School of Linguistics.

Langer, E. J., Blank, A., & Chanowitz, B. (1978). The mindlessness of ostensibly thoughtful action: The role of "placebic" information in interpersonal interaction. Journal of Personality and Social Psychology, 36(6), 635.

Brehm, J. W. (1966). A theory of psychological reactance.

Gueguen, N., & Pascual, A. (2000). Evocation of freedom and compliance: The "but you are free of…" technique. Current Research in Social Psychology, 5(18), 264-270.

Grant, A. M., & Hofmann, D. A. (2011). It's not all about me: Motivating hand hygiene among health care professionals by focusing on patients. Psychological Science, 22(12), 1494-1499.

Rucker, D. D., Petty, R. E., & Briñol, P. (2008). What's in a frame anyway?: A metacognitive analysis of the impact of one versus two-sided message framing on attitude certainty.

Journal of Consumer Psychology, 18(2), 137-149.

Petty, R. E., Cacioppo, J. T., & Heesacker, M. (1981). Effects of rhetorical questions on persuasion: A cognitive response analysis. Journal of Personality and Social Psychology, 40(3), 432.

Coulter, K. S., & Coulter, R. A. (2005). Size does matter: The effects of magnitude representation congruency on price perceptions and purchase likelihood. Journal of Consumer Psychology, 15(1), 64-76.

King, D., & Auschaitrakul, S. (2020). Symbolic sequence effects on consumers' judgments of truth for brand claims. Journal of Consumer Psychology, 30(2), 304-313.

Matlock, T. (2011). The conceptual motivation of aspect. Motivation in Grammar and the Lexicon, 27, 133.

Berger, J., Kim, Y. D., & Meyer, R. (2021). What makes content engaging? How emotional dynamics shape success. Journal of Consumer Research, 48(2), 235-250.

About the Author

Akash Jaiswal is a seasoned Customer Success Professional in Semiconductor Industry, known for his expertise in understanding customer perspectives and product persuasion. With a rich background in marketing, branding, advertising, and copywriting, Akash brings a unique blend of practical experience and innovative thinking to the field. His insights into Go-To-Market strategies and sales funnels are not just theoretical but born from hands-on involvement in guiding businesses towards growth and success.

Akash's journey in the world of marketing and customer engagement is a testament to his dedication and skill in helping businesses find their footing in the increasingly digital landscape. His approach goes beyond mere strategy; he assists companies in gaining the confidence they need to embark on their journey toward online business growth. His passion for creativity is not just a professional asset but a guiding force that inspires others to start their own journeys in marketing.

"Zero to Everyone" is Akash's second book, following the successful release of his debut, "I Too Can Create." In this latest work, he distills his extensive experience into actionable insights, aiming to empower entrepreneurs and marketers alike. His writing reflects a deep understanding of the market's nuances and an unwavering commitment to helping others achieve their marketing goals. Through his books, Akash continues to influence and shape the way businesses approach customer engagement and market penetration.